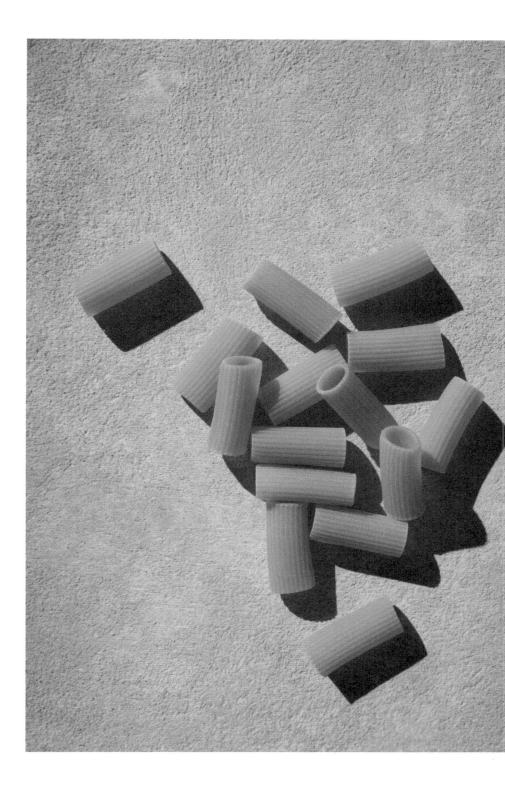

PASTA PRONTO!

THE PASTA MAN MATEO ZIELONKA

Simple, speedy recipes to make again & again

Photography by Matt Russell

Quadrille

INTRODUCTION

I've eaten a pasta dinner at least once or even twice a week pretty much all my life. I imagine that may be true for a lot of people, as pasta is incredibly popular – tasty, versatile, nutritious, it can be bought or made in a huge variety of shapes and cooked with different sauces to suit everyone. Whether it's a simple plate of pasta *al pesto*, a rich macaroni cheese with crunchy breadcrumb topping, a chunky minestrone soup, a bowl of spaghetti in tomato sauce – the options are endless.

Several years ago, I worked at a pasta restaurant in London. I was often stationed at a large table by the window overlooking the street, rolling out sheets of dough to cut into *tagliarini* or *fettucine*. Each day, I would watch hundreds of hungry people queueing outside the door and they in turn would watch their pasta being made. The window was like a small theatre and I felt like a magician entertaining a crowd.

I started to make fresh pasta at home a couple of years later, using a small domestic pasta machine that I picked up quite cheaply. I found a local shop that sold beautiful Italian flour and started to enjoy the rhythm of making dough by hand, rolling it and learning how to make new shapes. Pasta became my happy place and something of an obsession.

I began to post videos of pasta-shaping techniques online as a way of connecting with people who shared my passion. I made dozens of different pasta shapes, from *agnolini* to *ziti*, multicoloured ribbon pastas, playfully striped *cappelletti* or *ravioli*. It was a wonderful way to learn, as the warm responses I got meant that I kept exploring new methods and recipes. Somewhere along the way, I acquired the nickname The Pasta Man, which later became the title of my first cookbook. I couldn't have been more excited about it, not only because it's a such a joy to share my recipes, but because as a kid with dyslexia I was often written off as a bit slow. It was only later that I discovered I could find my way in life by focusing on my creativity, which found its expression in the kitchen.

Of course, making fresh pasta is probably not something you want to do every day of the week (okay, I do, but pasta is always on the menu at 180 Strand, in London, where I am head chef). It's surprisingly easy to make and – like anything – the more you practise, the quicker you'll be, so it's not out of the question to have fresh pasta for a midweek supper. That said, keeping a couple of packets of dried pasta in the kitchen cupboard means there's always an easy alternative, if you prefer.

Some days, you might be so tired that you just don't fancy cooking anything much and you want to turn to easy comfort food, something hot and satisfying that doesn't take too long to prepare. You get home from work and wish you'd thought to stop off at the shops, but a meeting ran late or the traffic was bad. This is what I call a 'pasta situation'. But if you're clever, a tasty bowl of pasta can be rustled up from ingredients that you have in the storecupboard.

I always keep a string of garlic in the kitchen, another of onions, a couple of lemons, a red chilli or two, good olive oil, canned tomatoes and a hunk of Parmesan. The freezer is handy too – for tomato sauce, garden peas, frozen herbs, all useful for conjuring up something *pronto*! I like to make wild garlic pesto in the spring and basil pesto in summertime, then I freeze it in small pots to use in the colder months. I grow flat-leaf parsley in the veg patch and copy my grandad's habit of chopping big bunches of parsley to keep in the freezer. (He used to freeze it in a blue ice-cream tub, and it tricked me on more than one occasion when I was a kid, expecting to steal a scoop of Neopolitan ice cream only to peel off the lid and find a boxful of chopped parsley instead!)

With a little bit of planning, lunch or dinner doesn't have to take long to make. It's the thinking about what to eat that often gets to you, not the actual cooking, as that can be a soothing activity, a change of pace after a busy day. Peeling and chopping a few vegetables, garlic sizzling in hot oil, the delicious scent of cheese bubbling under the grill (broiler); all of these hold the promise that something good to eat is coming.

I hope that the recipes in this book will help take some of the challenge out of planning what's for dinner. Tag a few pages, jot down your shopping list, stock up the kitchen cupboard and enjoy making some pasta. Make it often enough and it will soon become pasta *pronto*!

Mateo

BEFORE YOU START

Most of the recipes in this book can be made using either fresh or dried pasta – I've given options for both. Sometimes, using a dried pasta is simply a better choice and where that's the case, for example in a pasta salad, which benefits from the extra bite of dried pasta, I don't suggest an alternative. If you're making a filled *ravioli*, then of course you're going to have to start with a fresh pasta dough.

I make 100g/3½oz of fresh pasta per person, but generally weigh out 90g/3¼oz for each person if I'm using dried. I find these portions provide a satisfying meal, but if you have hungry teenagers in the house, then they can probably eat more (they can always eat more!), so adjust based on your own experience.

You might think that making fresh pasta is a step too far for a weekday dinner, but if you make the dough in a food processor it's surprisingly quick. Better still, make the dough a day or two ahead and leave it in the fridge, or make a big batch and freeze it in portions for two or four – the dough will keep for up to a month in the freezer (see page 17).

If you don't have time to make your own, look out for some of the fresh artisan pastas often available at good delicatessens or farmers' markets. Otherwise, simply use dried pasta. I have a drawerful of dried pasta in the kitchen – I'm a compulsive pasta shopper. There's always *orzo*, *spaghetti* and *messicani*; usually *linguine*, *rigatoni* and *mafaldine*; sometimes *radiatori* or *cresta di gallo* (cock's comb – the latter two are especially good in soups. In this book, however, I've tried to keep it simple, so I've used four ribbon pastas (*fettucine*, *tagliarini*, *pappardelle* and *spaghetti*) and four short pastas (*farfalle*, *cavatelli*, *rigatoni* and *orzo*). You can swap in your own ribbon or short shapes, depending on what your favourites are.

If you've made fresh pasta before, you can dive right in and start cooking, but if it's new to you, you may want to read on for a few tips about the pasta storecupboard and the equipment that you will need. You may prefer to save learning about making fresh pasta (pages 19–27) for when you've got a bit more time on your hands.

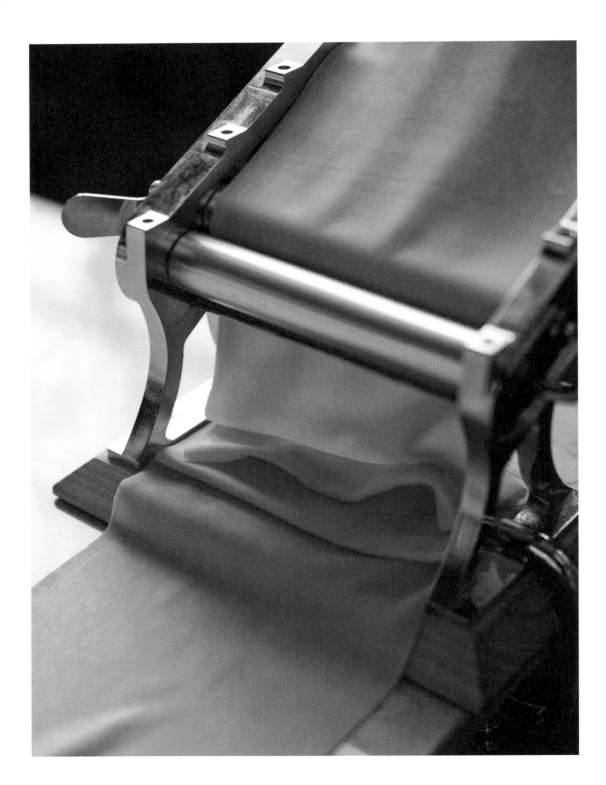

KITCHEN EQUIPMENT

PASTA MACHINE

When I first made pasta at home I started with a basic machine, a bit tinny but perfectly functional. Then I was hooked, so I upgraded to a better-quality brand, Marcato Atlas, which I've been using for years. Maybe put it on your birthday or Christmas wish list, or treat yourself. One thing to stress – do not wash your pasta machine. Let it dry out after use, then clean with a soft brush or a damp cloth. If you wash it, any flour that remains will act like glue, completely clogging up the machine.

FOOD PROCESSOR OR MINI CHOPPER

I've found that making pasta dough in a food processor is very quick and easy. I was surprised to find you can make enough dough to serve four in a mini chopper too – it's bigger than you think. Using an appliance is perhaps not as relaxing as making dough by hand, but if you're trying to get dinner on the table *pronto*, as a short cut it's great. Either one is also useful for whizzing up pesto or sauces, or for making *Pangrattato* (page 146).

KITCHENAID

If you have a stand mixer, you can also use it to make pasta dough. If you buy the extra pasta attachment, you can roll out the dough too – even better. KitchenAid (as well as other well-known brands of stand mixer) sell a bundle that includes the roller plus two cutters, which make *fettucine* and *tagliarini*, so you're all ready to go. A bonus is that the attachments take up less space than a chunky pasta machine, as they can be stored in a small box.

RAVIOLI CUTTER

If you'd like a fancy zigzag edge to your *ravioli*, you need to buy a *ravioli* cutter with a brass cutting wheel. This seals the edges of the pasta as well as cutting it, so it's more sophisticated than a pastry wheel (and much sharper, too). Bear in mind that a *ravioli* cutter shouldn't be washed. Allow it to dry, then brush off any remaining flour with a soft brush or a cloth.

CHITARRA BOX

If you'd like to make fresh spaghetti at home, you'll need a *chittara* box. This is a wooden frame with thin wire strings stretched across it, and it comes with a small rolling pin to push the rolled pasta dough through the strings to make the *spaghetti* shape. It is quite an extravagance, but if you're a *spaghetti* fan it may be worth investing in one. Look online to source one, but bear in mind they are bulky to store, and they only make one pasta shape.

KITCHEN KNIFE

A good, sharp kitchen knife is best for cutting pasta dough cleanly. It's not good to pull the dough out of shape by tearing it with a blunt blade.

LARGE SAUCEPAN FOR COOKING PASTA

I'm not talking about a specialist pasta pan here, just a pan that's large enough to let the pasta cook well. If the pasta clumps together in a pan that's too small, it will cook unevenly. At home, I use a stainless-steel, 6-litre/12½-pint pan.

WIDE SAUCEPAN FOR SAUCES

This may sound picky, but I really do recommend cooking sauces in a wide saucepan. Mine is around 25cm/10in across and about 8cm/3in deep. It's best to transfer the cooked pasta to the sauce, so you need room to combine the two, and a large, relatively shallow saucepan is the way to go.

PARMESAN GRATER

I'm a big fan of Microplane graters. A sharp, precise, rasp grater is perfect for hard cheese and is an elegant grater to bring to the table with a chunk of Parmesan.

THE PASTA STORECUPBOARD

ITALIAN 00 FLOUR

Finely milled flour that has been ground twice to give the lightest texture, 00 flour creates a beautifully smooth, pliable dough. Look out for the high-quality flour made by Molino Pasini near Modena, northern Italy. We are lucky to have a local stockist in Dorset, Mercato Italiano, so you may be able to track it down wherever you are, too.

FINE SEMOLINA

Sometimes known as *semola rimacinata*, fine semolina is ground from durum wheat and is used to make vegan pasta dough.

I use coarse semolina for dusting pasta dough, either to dry out the pasta while working it, if needed, or to prevent the pasta sticking together after it's been shaped. To keep things simple in this book, I've suggested you use fine semolina instead, as it does the job just as well. Rice flour is a good alternative, too.

EGGS

I use free-range, rich-yolk eggs, when I can get them, as they give an attractive golden tone to the pasta dough. The most important thing is to buy good-quality eggs from hens reared to high welfare standards. I've given two ways of making egg dough in this book. One is a Classic Pasta Dough (page 19); the second uses extra egg yolks, which produces a richer colour and a dough that I find easier to roll (see Rich Egg Dough, page 22). The downside is that you will end up with leftover egg whites, so you may want to brush up on your baking skills. My partner likes to bake friends, so we have a ready-made solution: eat more cake.

I always use medium eggs in my recipes. They weigh around 50g/2oz, if anyone's wanting to get technical.

DRIED PASTA

When you buy dried pasta, choose one that is made with durum wheat and water, which will be labelled 'bronze extruded' or '*trafila ruvida al bronzo*'. This means that the pasta is formed through a bronze die, giving it a rough, porous surface, which helps it to carry the sauce. My favourite brands are Garofolo and De Cecco, which can easily be found in a good grocery store or supermarket. Voiello is another quality brand to look out for. I brought home a packet of their *spaghettini* from a wonderful food emporium in Naples, which was stacked from floor to ceiling with pasta, wheels of Parmesan and wine. Heaven.

OLIVE OIL

I love to cook with olive oil, but it has become very expensive, perhaps understandably so. You can use half-and-half olive oil and a good-quality vegetable oil to cook sauces, saving your best olive oil to finish a dish or to make salad dressings, where the flavour is more prominent. I can still fall for a beautiful, graphic olive oil can to keep on the kitchen shelf; some brands really know how to seduce you with eye-catching designs.

PARMESAN AND PECORINO

Grainy, complex and sharp, Parmesan cheese is used to finish pasta dishes and is occasionally cooked in pasta sauces. Look out for *Parmigiano Reggiano*, which is the authentic cow's milk cheese from northern Italy that is aged for a minimum of 12 months. Parmesan is also available as a vegetarian cheese made without animal rennet and is usually stocked in good supermarkets or specialist cheese shops.

Pecorino, a hard sheep's milk cheese, has a softer flavour and a slightly creamier texture than Parmesan and can be used as an alternative. Purists may disagree, but it's up to you which you prefer.

Save any leftover Parmesan or pecorino rinds and freeze them. I like to use them in *Pasta e Ceci* (page 119) or *pasta e fagioli*, *béchamel* or *risotto*.

SALT AND PEPPER

Pasta needs salt for flavour, just as potatoes do. I use table salt in pasta cooking water because it's cheap and does the job. I always use sea salt flakes to finish a dish; sometimes that extra salty crunch is just what's needed.

Pepper is always freshly ground black pepper.

Note that I only give seasoning quantities in recipes where a particular amount is required; otherwise I think it's best left to your own personal taste. Always check the seasoning before you serve the finished dish.

OTHER STAPLES

Other kitchen staples for me include **lemons**, a jar of **anchovies in oil**, **onions**, a few bulbs of **garlic**, **chilli (hot pepper) flakes** – any of these in various combinations will make a simple pasta sauce for a quick midweek supper. I also have several tins of **tomatoes** and **tomato purée (paste)** in the cupboard, as well as jars of **white beans** and **chickpeas (garbanzo beans)**. I keep a box of **chopped parsley** in the freezer and in summer a pot of **fresh basil** is always on the kitchen windowsill.

HOW TO COOK PASTA

If you've read my previous books, *The Pasta Man* or *Pasta Masterclass*, then you'll be familiar with these pasta cooking tips. If not, read on. Follow these steps and you'll soon be cooking pasta like a pro!

THE COOKING WATER

Use a large saucepan to cook your fresh pasta. The water should be able to circulate around the pasta, otherwise it will not cook evenly and can clump together.

Season the water heavily. Pasta is made from flour and egg, or semolina and water, so any seasoning is absorbed from the cooking water and from the sauce it's served with. I add table salt to season the water once it is boiling (if you add salt to cold water, it simply takes longer to boil). I don't recommend a particular quantity of salt – they vary in flavour and intensity – but the water should taste as salty as sea water.

COOKING FRESH OR DRIED PASTA

Always drop the pasta into the water once it's boiling steadily. If you're impatient and add it too soon, the pasta won't cook perfectly.

Super-fresh pasta cooks very quickly. If you cook the pasta as soon you've shaped it, it may only take 1 minute to cook. If you shaped it a day or two ahead, then it might take 2–3 minutes to cook. Scoop a piece out and taste it before you drain the pan.

For dried pastas, follow the cooking time on the packet, but check it a minute or two before the time stated. I like the pasta to be a little *al dente* and it will finish cooking in the accompanying sauce anyway.

Make sure that your sauce is hot and ready a minute before your pasta is cooked. As fresh pasta cooks so quickly, the sauce should be hot at the same time as you drop the pasta into the boiling water. For dried pastas, return the sauce to the heat a couple of minutes before the pasta is *al dente*.

Don't leave pasta sitting in the cooking water. Drain it straight away, either by tipping it into a colander or sieve (strainer), always making sure you keep a jugful of the starchy cooking water, as you may need it to loosen the sauce.

COOKING FILLED PASTA

If you've made a large quantity of *ravioli*, you may find it easier to cook the pasta in two batches, one after the other, transferring each batch to the sauce once cooked.

Lift the *ravioli* out of the water using a slotted spoon, reserving the pasta cooking water until you've combined the pasta with the sauce. The sauce may need loosening, but add water a little at a time, moving the pasta gently around the pan, so that the *ravioli* parcels don't split.

FREEZING PASTA

You can freeze pasta dough for up to a month wrapped tightly in clingfilm (plastic wrap). Take it out of the freezer the evening before you want to use it and leave it to slowly defrost in the fridge. The dough will have a slightly different consistency when you come to roll it, but don't worry – if it crumbles as you first put it through the machine, simply bring it together with your hands, press together and then try rolling it again.

I never freeze ribbon pasta, as the strands tend to become brittle and then break when cooked from frozen. I only really recommend freezing filled pastas. Filled pastas are best if they are blanched before freezing, as they will keep longer; it's a chore but it does work. Blanch in boiling seasoned water for 10 seconds, then plunge into iced water straight away. Drain, leave to cool and dry out a little, then place on a tray lined with baking parchment. Freeze on the tray, so that the filled pasta freeze as individual pieces, then transfer them to a container. To cook, simply drop the frozen pasta into boiling salted water and allow an extra minute's cooking time.

CLASSIC PASTA DOUGH

This is the classic recipe for fresh pasta, using whole eggs and Italian 00 flour. If you can buy eggs labelled free-range *and* rich yolk, then your pasta will have a lovely golden hue, but even using ordinary free-range eggs will give you a soft yellow dough, ready to shape into ribbon pastas like *tagliarini* or *fettucine*, or to make into plump *ravioli* parcels wrapped around a savoury filling.

MAKES 400G/14OZ, ENOUGH TO SERVE 4

300g/10½oz Italian 00 flour, plus extra, if needed

3 medium eggs

TO MAKE WITH A FOOD PROCESSOR

The quickest way to make the dough is using a food processor. I love to make pasta by hand, especially at home; I find it a mindful, soothing activity. But sometimes time is not on your side, so this is something of a chef's cheat (just don't tell your *nonna*).

Add the flour to the processor bowl and crack the eggs over the top. Secure the lid and start the machine. Mix for 30 seconds until the dough has the consistency of fine breadcrumbs, or until it starts to come together.

The texture of the dough will depend on the size of the eggs you use, and egg sizes vary considerably, so if the dough is too moist, add a level tablespoon of 00 flour and mix for another 10 seconds. If the dough is too dry and crumbly, add a teaspoon of water and mix for another 10 seconds.

Transfer the mixture to a mixing bowl and use your hands to bring it together to form a neat disc of dough (this will make it easier to roll out later).

Place the dough in an airtight container and let it rest in the fridge for a minimum of 30 minutes. If you want to prep ahead, you can leave the dough in the fridge for up to 48 hours, but if you do this, I find it's better to wrap the dough tightly in clingfilm (plastic wrap) to stop it drying out.

TO MAKE WITH A STAND MIXER

If you have a stand mixer (such as a KitchenAid), this is another great way to speed up the process of making pasta dough. It will still take 10 minutes of kneading, but the machine does all the work, while you can get on with assembling and cooking the ingredients for a sauce or pasta filling.

Fit the dough hook attachment to your mixer. Add the flour and eggs to the bowl and turn to setting 2 (if you start on a high speed, you'll probably get a small explosion of flour all over you). After about 2 minutes, once the flour has combined with

the egg, increase to setting 4 and mix steadily for another 5–7 minutes.

By now, the dough will have come together and will look smooth. I find that there are fewer issues with the hydration of the dough using a stand mixer, but if yours is on the dry side, add 1 teaspoon of tepid water and mix for another minute.

Lift the dough onto the work surface and slightly flatten to a disc shape (this will make it easier to roll out later). Place it in an airtight container and put it in the fridge for a minimum of 30 minutes. You can leave the dough in the fridge for up to 48 hours if you want to prep ahead, but if you do this, I find it's better to wrap the dough tightly in clingfilm (plastic wrap) to stop it drying out.

TO MAKE BY HAND

This is 10 minutes of mindfulness to me – a happy workout – so even if I want to have dinner on the table quickly, I may still make my pasta dough by hand. Like anything, the more you do it, the easier it becomes. I call it my pasta auto-pilot mode.

Place the flour on a clean work surface or board and shape it into a mound. Make a well in the centre and crack the eggs into the middle.

Using a fork, break the eggs yolks and start to gently whisk them. Draw in the flour a little at a time and continue to combine with the fork.

When everything starts to come together, use your hands to knead the dough and continue to knead for 8–10 minutes until smooth. Use the heel of your hand and push away from you, using your other hand to turn the dough 90 degrees after each knead – you will soon develop a lovely rhythm.

If you find that the dough feels a little stiff and difficult to work with, keep going, as it will become more elastic the more you work it. Alternatively, leave the dough on the work surface, place a bowl over it and come back to it after 5 minutes. This will soften the dough and make it easier to knead.

When the dough is smooth, form it into a flat disc (this will make it easier to roll out later). Place it in an airtight container and put it in the fridge for a minimum of 30 minutes. You can leave the dough in the fridge for up to 48 hours if you want to prep ahead, but if you do I find it's better to wrap the dough tightly in clingfilm (plastic wrap) to prevent it drying out.

RICH EGG DOUGH

This is my favourite pasta dough recipe. I use it all the time at work, but it is a little extravagant to use a half-dozen eggs to serve four people, so if you're making a family supper, I'd stick to Classic Pasta Dough (page 19).

I find that rich egg dough, made using egg yolks as well as whole eggs, creates a firmer, more pliable and more consistent dough. If you can, hunt down eggs that are labelled rich yolk, as they really do make a difference to the colour and texture of the pasta.

Use the leftover egg whites to make friands, meringues or pavlova, or add to scrambled eggs, and remember that you can freeze egg whites, too.

MAKES 400G/14OZ, ENOUGH TO SERVE 4

280g/10oz Italian 00 flour, plus extra,
   if needed

2 whole eggs, plus 4 egg yolks

TO MAKE WITH A FOOD PROCESSOR

Add the flour to the processor bowl and crack the eggs and yolks over the top. Secure the lid and start the machine. Mix for 30 seconds until the dough has the consistency of fine breadcrumbs, or until it starts to come together.

The texture of the dough will depend on the size of the eggs you use, and egg sizes vary considerably, so if the dough is too moist, add a level tablespoon of 00 flour and mix for another 10 seconds. If the dough is too dry and crumbly, add a teaspoon of water and mix for another 10 seconds.

Transfer the mixture to a mixing bowl and use your hands to bring it together to form a neat disc of dough (this will make it easier to roll out later).

Place the dough in an airtight container and let it rest in the fridge for a minimum of 30 minutes. If you want to prep ahead, you can leave the dough in the fridge for up to 48 hours, but if you do this, I find it's better to wrap the dough tightly in clingfilm (plastic wrap) to stop it drying out.

TO MAKE WITH A STAND MIXER

Fit the dough hook attachment to your mixer. Add the flour and eggs to the bowl and turn to setting 2 (if you start on a high speed, you'll probably get a small explosion of flour all over you). After about 2 minutes, once the flour has combined with the egg, increase to setting 4 and mix steadily for another 5–7 minutes.

By now, the dough will have come together and will look smooth. I find that there are fewer issues with the hydration of the dough using a stand mixer, but if yours is on the dry side, add 1 teaspoon tepid water and mix for another minute.

Lift the dough onto the work surface and slightly flatten to a disc shape (this will make it easier to roll out later). Place it in an airtight container and refrigerate, as described on page 22.

TO MAKE BY HAND

Place the flour on a clean work surface or board and shape it into a mound. Make a well in the centre, crack the eggs into the middle and add the extra egg yolks.

Using a fork, break the eggs yolks and start to gently whisk them. Draw in the flour a little at a time and continue to combine with the fork.

When everything starts to come together, use your hands to knead the dough and continue to knead for 8–10 minutes until smooth. Use the heel of your hand and push away from you, using your other hand to turn the dough 90 degrees after each knead – you will soon develop a lovely rhythm.

If you find that the dough feels a little stiff and difficult to work with, keep going, as it will become more elastic the more you work it. Alternatively, leave the dough on the work surface, place a bowl over it and come back to it after 5 minutes. This will soften the dough and make it easier to knead.

When the dough is smooth, form it into a flat disc (this will make it easier to roll out later). Place it in an airtight container and refrigerate, as described on page 22.

GLUTEN-FREE EGG DOUGH

This gluten-free egg dough is good to use for either ribbon or filled pastas. Using xanthum gum as a stabilizer means that the dough won't crumble, even though there's no gluten to bind the flours together. I like to mix chickpea (gram) and rice flours; the flavour is ever so slightly nutty, but as close to a classic pasta dough as it could be. You need to handle the dough carefully when you're rolling it out, as it can be a little fragile, but it seems to be more robust when you come to shaping it.

MAKES 400G/14OZ, ENOUGH TO SERVE 4

210g/7½oz chickpea (gram) flour

90g/3¼oz rice flour

1½ teaspoons xanthum gum

3 whole eggs, plus 1 egg yolk

TO MAKE WITH A FOOD PROCESSOR

Combine the dry ingredients in a bowl, making sure the xanthum gum is evenly mixed in. Transfer to the bowl of the food processor, then add the eggs and yolk and mix for 30 seconds until the dough comes together.

Return to the clean bowl and press the mixture to form a neat disc.

It's best to wrap this dough in clingfilm (plastic wrap). I find it can dry out slightly in an airtight container, and it's essential to keep the moisture in this dough to make it easier to roll. Chill the dough in the fridge for a minimum of 30 minutes before shaping. If you like, you can make the dough a day or two ahead, as it will sit quite happily in the fridge for up to 48 hours.

TO MAKE BY HAND

Combine the flours in a bowl, add the xanthum gum and then tip out onto a clean work surface or board and shape into a mound. Make a well in the centre and crack the eggs and yolk into the middle.

Using a fork, break the egg yolks and start to gently whisk them. Draw in the flour a little at a time and continue to combine with the fork.

When everything starts to come together, use your hands to knead the dough. Continue to knead for 3–5 minutes until smooth (you don't knead it for as long as the Classic Pasta Dough, as you're not developing the gluten here).

Wrap the dough in clingfilm (plastic wrap) and chill as above.

VEGAN SEMOLINA DOUGH

This fresh egg-free dough is made from the same two ingredients as shop-bought dried pasta: durum wheat and water. The only difference is in the proportion of the ingredients used. Commercial dough is passed through an extruder, which can make dozens of different pasta shapes, whereas homemade semolina dough is usually used for simple shapes made by hand.

Fine semolina is a type of flour ground from durum wheat, milled twice to produce a fine texture, which in turn produces a fine-textured dough. When the dough is cooked it has more bite than softer egg pasta, and it also takes slightly longer to cook, around 5–6 minutes. I like to serve this type of pasta with robust flavours, such as ragù or a rich cheese sauce.

280g/10oz fine semolina
130ml/generous ½ cup warm water

TO MAKE WITH A STAND MIXER

Use the dough hook attachment on your mixer. Add the semolina and water to the bowl and mix on setting 2 until the semolina and water are blended. Increase to setting 4, then mix steadily until the dough is formed, about 5–7 minutes.

Lift the dough onto the work surface and slightly flatten into a disc shape. There's no need to rest semolina dough – it can be used straight away – but if you want to prep ahead, you can wrap it in clingfilm (plastic wrap) or place it in an airtight container in the fridge for up to 48 hours.

TO MAKE BY HAND

Add the semolina to a large mixing bowl and pour the warm water all over it. Combine with a fork until it looks like a crumble mix, then start to form the dough into a loose ball with your hands.

As soon as the dough has come together, turn it onto a clean work surface or board and start to knead until it is smooth and feels elastic; this will take about 10 minutes. Use the heel of your hand and push away from you, then use the other hand to turn the dough 90 degrees and repeat. You will soon develop a lovely rhythm.

When the dough is smooth, form it into a flat disc and place it in an airtight container until you're ready to shape your pasta.

DOUGH
ROLL
SHAPE

HOW TO ROLL PASTA DOUGH

WITH A PASTA MACHINE

I use several different pasta machines at work and at home, but the settings I've used in this book are based on a Marcato Atlas, a popular Italian brand. The widest setting on the Marcato is 0, but on the Imperia it's 6, and on a KitchenAid or Pastalinda it's 1. To make it easy to refer to the settings for each of these machines, here's a handy chart showing you which settings to roll to for either ribbon or filled pastas.

Brand	Marcato Atlas	KitchenAid	Pastalinda	Imperia
Settings from wide to narrow	0–8	1–8	1–9	6–1
For ribbon pastas	5–6	6	8	2
For filled pastas	6–7	7–8	9	1

This is the rolling technique that you'll need to refer to if you're making any of the fresh pasta shapes in this book. Once you've done it a few times, it will become a habit and you'll be so familiar with the settings on your machine that you won't need to reread this.

To start rolling, cut about a quarter from the disc of pasta dough, flatten it a little and guide it through the widest setting on your pasta machine twice (on my machine this is 0).

Move to the next widest setting (on my machine this is 1), then take the dough through this setting twice.

Now click back to the widest setting. Fold the dough in half from end to end, flatten it slightly and roll it through the machine twice again.

Click to the next widest setting (you're now on 1 again). Roll the dough through the machine twice.

Continue to guide the dough twice through each setting. If you are making long ribbon pastas – *tagliarini*, *fettucine* or *pappardelle* – stop rolling at setting 5 or 6, depending on how thick you like your pasta. If you're making filled pasta, such as *ravioli*, you want the dough to be finer, so stop rolling on setting 7.

If you find that the pasta is too sticky and proves difficult to roll out, gently dust it with 00 flour (the same flour you used to make the dough). Pat it lightly over the surface, so that the dough just absorbs the flour, then you should be able to continue.

WITH A KITCHENAID

If you already have a KitchenAid (or other stand mixer) and enjoy fresh homemade pasta, then I recommend buying the pasta attachment, which makes it so easy to roll out sheets of dough. You can buy a bundle that includes a roller and two cutters to make *fettucine* and *tagliarini* – ribbon pastas that everyone loves twirling around their fork like a proper Italian.

The KitchenAid runs at different speeds to suit your experience. The first time you use the pasta attachment, start on setting 3. If you go any higher, the pasta will roll out of the machine alarmingly fast! Save that for when you're feeling like a pro.

Start by cutting about a quarter from the disc of pasta dough, then flatten it a little and guide it through the widest setting (1) twice.

Move to the next widest setting (2), then take the dough through this setting twice.

Now click back to the widest setting (1). Fold the dough in half from end to end, flatten it slightly and turn it 90 degrees. Roll it through the machine again twice. The reason for turning the dough is to create as wide a rectangle as possible.

Click to the next widest setting (2). Roll the dough through the machine twice.

Continue to guide the dough twice through each setting. If you are making long ribbon pastas – *tagliarini*, *fettucine* or *pappardelle* – stop rolling at setting 6. If you are making filled pasta such as *ravioli*, you want the dough to be finer, so stop rolling on setting 7. If you like really thin, delicate pasta, then roll to setting 8.

DOUGH
ROLL
SHAPE

The pasta shapes I've suggested here are easy to cut with a pasta machine attachment or to shape by hand; there are no fancy techniques involved. When you're confident and feel like trying something more challenging, you can make more complex shapes. There are plenty of options to try in my book *Pasta Masterclass*. Or look online at Mateo.Kitchen, where you can follow videos to help with different shaping techniques for dozens of different pastas.

FETTUCINE AND TAGLIARINI

Equipment: pasta machine or KitchenAid with cutter attachment

A pasta machine with a cutting attachment makes these shapes very easy to make. They're a good place to start if you're just learning how to use your pasta machine or KitchenAid attachments. Both pastas are versatile and pair well with all sorts of sauces.

METHOD

Prepare a tray or baking sheet dusted with fine semolina or rice flour, ready to lay out your finished pasta.

Start with half the dough, leaving the other half wrapped until you're ready to use it.

Following the method on page 29, roll out the pasta dough, stopping at setting 5 or 6, depending on how thin you like your pasta. I like more bite, so I usually stop at setting 5, but remember to check the settings for your own machine on page 29. Cut the sheets into 25cm/10in lengths using a sharp kitchen knife.

Attach the pasta cutter to your machine and guide the sheets through on the relevant cutter. Dust the cut pasta with semolina and either lay it flat on the tray or lift it by the centre of the strands and curl into individual nests, or hang it from a pasta drying rack.

If you're using a KitchenAid to cut the pasta, you will need to remove the rolling attachment and replace it with the *fettucine* or *tagliariani* attachment. Turn on the KitchenAid (start with setting 3, don't go too fast) and feed the pasta sheet through the cutter. Dust the cut pasta with semolina and lay it on the prepared tray.

You can leave the pasta to dry a little, if you like, but if you are cutting the pasta more than an hour ahead of cooking, remember to cover the whole tray with a dish towel to keep it from drying out too much. It's fine to use it straight away, but remember that it will cook faster, so you may need to adjust the cooking time. Nobody likes soggy pasta.

If you are shaping the pasta a day ahead of cooking it, dust it with fine semolina or rice flour and store in an airtight container in the fridge.

PAPPARDELLE
Equipment: kitchen knife

This is one of my favourite pastas, as I like the chunky cut of the ribbons, which carry lots of sauce. *Pappardelle* with gorgonzola and speck? Yes chef! This shape is cut with a kitchen knife; just make sure you use one with a sharp blade.

METHOD
Start with half the dough, leaving the other half wrapped until you're ready to use it, and have ready a tray or baking sheet dusted with fine semolina or rice flour ready for your finished pasta.

Roll out the dough (page 29), stopping at setting 5 or 6, depending on how thick you like your pasta.

Cut the sheets into lengths using a sharp kitchen knife – I like to do mine around 15–20cm/6–8in long – then dust each sheet with fine semolina or rice flour and stack them on top of one another. The aim is to produce a neat pile like a stack of playing cards.

When you've finished rolling the first half of the dough, fold the whole stack of sheets in half and turn the fold towards you.

Using a sharp knife, cut the sheets into ribbons about 3cm/1¼in wide.

Carefully lift each bundle of cut pasta and gently shake off the semolina (some will still cling to the strands, but that's okay). Lay them in piles or folds on the tray, cover with a dish towel and then roll out the other half of the dough.

You can cook the pasta straight away, if you like, but remember to adjust the cooking time as super-fresh pasta will cook more quickly. Otherwise, leave the pasta for about 30 minutes, so that it dries out slightly before cooking.

If you are cutting the pasta more than an hour ahead of cooking, cover the whole tray with a dish towel to stop it drying out too much. If you are shaping it a day ahead of cooking, then turn each stack of *pappardelle* onto the cut side (which stops them from compacting), dust each one with fine semolina or rice flour and store in an airtight container in the fridge.

SPAGHETTI ALLA CHITARRA
Equipment: *chitarra* box

You can't make *spaghetti* with a pasta machine attachment, so you need a *chitarra* box. It's something of an investment, but *spaghetti* is always a big favourite and it's fun to make it. The thin wire strings of the *chitarra* box are stretched across a wooden frame, a lot like a guitar, which is where the name actually comes from. The cutter comes with a small rolling pin to push the rolled pasta dough through the strings to make the shape known as *spaghetti alla chitarra*.

You can make *chitarra* using either egg or vegan dough, but I tend to use the Classic Pasta Dough (page 19) as it's firmer and easier to work with. Of course, it's always an option to substitute fresh egg *spaghetti* with a shop-bought dried *spaghetti*, or you could swap the shape and make *tagliarini* or *fettucine* instead.

METHOD
Prepare a tray or baking sheet dusted with fine semolina or rice flour, ready to lay out your finished pasta.

Start rolling using half the dough, keeping the rest well wrapped until you're ready to use it. Roll out the pasta dough to setting 5 or 6, depending on how thick you like your pasta (page 29).

Cut the sheet into rectangles that are 5cm/2in shorter than the length of the *chitarra* box. Dust each sheet with fine semolina or rice flour and stack them as you cut them.

Place a pasta sheet on top of the box along the line of the strings and dust with more semolina. Using the rolling pin, roll it back and forth across the strings, so that the strands fall through them into the box below.

Take out the *chitarra* strands and place on the tray, either in straight lines or twisted into small nests. Roll out the rest of the dough and repeat.

You can leave the pasta to dry a little, if you like, but if you are cutting the pasta more than an hour ahead of cooking, cover the whole tray with a dish towel to keep it from drying out too much. It's fine to use it straight away, but remember that it will cook faster, so you may need to adjust the cooking time. If you are shaping the pasta a day ahead of cooking it, dust it with fine semolina or rice flour and store in an airtight container in the fridge.

FARFALLE

These little bow ties hold sauces very well. When I was a kid, my grandad always used to throw a handful into a tomato soup. The butterfly shape makes them *very* popular with children. Maybe get them to help you make supper, although I doubt it'll be *pronto*!

Equipment: *ravioli* cutter for fluted edges, or a sharp kitchen knife for plain edges

METHOD

Start with a quarter of the dough, keeping the rest well wrapped, and prepare a tray or baking sheet dusted with fine semolina or rice flour, ready to lay out your finished pasta.

Following the method on page 29, roll out the pasta dough, stopping at setting 5 or 6, depending on how thick you like your pasta.

Cut across the pasta sheet using the *ravioli* cutter or kitchen knife, spacing the cuts around 5cm/2in apart. Next, using the kitchen knife, cut lengthways at the same spacing to create squares. The squares will have the classic zigzag edges on two opposite sides and be straight-edged on the other two sides; if you've only used a knife, they will be straight on all four sides.

Place a square on the work surface with the zigzags to each side and the straight edges top and bottom. Place your index finger in the centre of the square to hold it steady, then slide your thumb and middle finger towards the middle, creating two ridges in the dough that you then pinch together. The dough will stick to form the butterfly shape.

Place the *farfalle* on the dusted tray and continue with the rest of the dough until you have a nice pile.

CAVATELLI

This is a shape made with semolina dough, a robust dough quite different to smooth egg pasta. There's a pleasing bite to semolina pastas. Rolled into ropes and cut into segments, each segment is shaped into a tiny curl with a small dip to capture the sauce. You use your thumb to make this shape – no fancy equipment, just a labour of love.

You don't need to rest the dough in the fridge before shaping, and you can use it straight away.

METHOD

Prepare a tray or baking sheet dusted with fine semolina or rice flour, ready to lay out your finished pasta.

Take about one quarter of the Vegan Semolina Dough (page 26), keeping the rest well wrapped, and roll into a long rope that is about the thickness of a pencil.

Cut the pasta into pieces about 1.5–2cm/¾in long. Now place a piece of dough on the work surface in front of you, press your thumb into the centre and drag the dough away from you, which will create a small curl, a bit like a butter curl. This does take some practice, but it is very satisfying once you get the hang of it. It's not a shape that relies on neat consistency; the look is rustic, which is lucky, because that's what you'll get.

Place the shapes on the tray while you roll and shape the rest of the dough.

RAVIOLI

Equipment: *ravioli* cutter with a fluted edge, or a sharp knife

This is the most well-known filled pasta shape. Who doesn't like cutting into a *ravioli* parcel to find out what's inside? It's an easy shape to make, but it can take a while if you're making enough for a crowd, so it's best to make *ravioli* when you've got some time on your hands. I think of it as weekend cooking, a treat for Saturday night supper.

METHOD

Have ready a tray or baking sheet dusted with fine semolina or rice flour for your finished shapes. Keep a glass of chilled water and a pastry brush to hand.

Bearing in mind that you need quite a bit of clear work surface space to make *ravioli*, start with about a quarter of the dough. Roll out sheets of dough up to setting 6 or 7, depending on what thickness of pasta you like (see page 29 for your machine settings).

Fold the sheet in half lengthways and press down lightly on the fold to mark the centre, then spread the sheet out flat again. Now drop teaspoons of filling just above the fold line, with a thumb-width space between each spoonful, until the length of the dough is filled.

Using the pastry brush or a finger, dab a tiny bit of water carefully around each spoonful of filling, then fold the dough over the filling, so that the long edges meet. Press together to seal. Now press down quite hard in between the little mounds of filling to seal each one, ready for cutting into individual pieces. Look out for any air pockets that may have formed and push the air away and out of the edges of the pasta – this will prevent the *ravioli* from splitting when you cook it.

The next part is fun. Using a *ravioli* cutter or a sharp knife, cut along the length of the dough and then in between each mound to create individual pieces of *ravioli*.

Lift each *ravioli* onto the dusted tray, then dust again with a little fine semolina or rice flour while you roll and fill the next batch of dough.

(See page 17 for freezing instructions.)

PRONTO PRONTO!

NINE QUICK WINS

Sometimes, you just want a proper hot meal that can be on the table inside 20 minutes and that will leave everyone feeling satisfied. These are the recipes I turn to when I'm in a hurry. I probably have most of the ingredients at home, but I may pick up a couple of lemons or a bag of spinach on the way back from work. Often, a little planning can go a long way, whether it's leaving some prawns (shrimp) to defrost while you're out at work or making sure you always have a few basics in stock, such as garlic, anchovies and chillies. Nearly everyone has a packet of *spaghetti* in the cupboard – you just need to cook a quick sauce to go with it, and if you make sure to keep a block of Parmesan or pecorino in the fridge, then supper is sorted – *pronto, pronto*!

SPAGHETTI WITH CREAMY RICOTTA AND BASIL

Ricotta makes a deliciously creamy yet light sauce, which is especially good when blended with fragrant basil leaves. Such a simple summer supper, served with a green leaf salad or a dish of Shaved Courgettes with Basil and Mint (see page 143) and a glass of chilled white wine.

SERVES 4

FRESH PASTA
400g/14oz *spaghetti alla chitarra* (page 37)

DRIED PASTA
360g/13oz dried *spaghetti*

45ml/3 tablespoons olive oil

2 garlic cloves, thinly sliced

2 shallots, thinly sliced

55g/2oz Parmesan (vegetarian, if necessary), grated

bunch of basil (about 25g/1oz), leaves only

zest of 1 lemon; juice of ½

200g/7oz ricotta

Pangrattato (page 146), to serve

Heat the olive oil in a large saucepan and fry the garlic and shallots on a medium heat until soft. This will take about 5 minutes. Set to one side.

Place the Parmesan, basil leaves, lemon zest and juice in the bowl of a food processor and blitz for 15–20 seconds until you have a thick paste. Transfer this mixture to a medium bowl, add the ricotta and use a wooden spoon to combine well. Season to taste with sea salt and freshly ground black pepper, then leave to one side while you cook the pasta.

Bring a large pan of water to the boil before adding salt, then cook the *spaghetti* for 1½–2 minutes. Alternatively, if using dried pasta, follow the packet instructions.

Once the pasta is cooked, use kitchen tongs to transfer it to the saucepan of shallots, carrying over some of the starchy cooking water. Stir together well, then add the ricotta mixture and continue to stir. Loosen the sauce with extra pasta cooking water, if needed. Check the seasoning and serve in four warmed bowls, scattering a generous handful of *Pangrattato* on top.

SPAGHETTI WITH ARTICHOKE HEARTS AND LEMON

I had an early start one morning in Rome and found myself in the market at Campo di Fiori, just as the stallholders were finishing setting up for the day. The beautiful displays of produce were so colourful and tempting and everyone seemed to be truly proud of the fruit, vegetables and herbs that they were selling. I watched a lady peeling *carciofi* (artichokes), then dropping the hearts into lemon water to stop them discolouring. I can still picture her dextrous handiwork when I make this *spaghetti* dish at home. Luckily, we can buy jars of artichoke hearts at the supermarket, which makes this a simple supper to prepare.

SERVES 4

FRESH PASTA
400g/14oz egg *spaghetti alla chitarra* (pages 37 and 22)

DRIED PASTA
360g/13oz dried *spaghetti*

1 x 300g/10½oz jar of artichoke hearts (in oil or water, either is good)

45ml/3 tablespoons olive oil

4 garlic cloves, finely chopped

50g/2oz butter

zest and juice of ½ lemon

handful of parsley, chopped

grated Parmesan or *Pangrattato* (page 146), to serve

Drain the artichokes, then cut into thin slices. (If you buy the hearts in oil, I tend not to use the oil to cook with, as it can be a little acidic.)

Heat the olive oil in a large saucepan, add the garlic and fry for 1 minute, then add the artichokes and fry on a low heat for 4 minutes, stirring occasionally.

Meanwhile, bring a large pan of water to the boil before adding salt, then cook the spaghetti for 1½–2 minutes. Alternatively, if using dried pasta, follow the packet instructions.

Use kitchen tongs to transfer the pasta to the sauce along with half a ladleful of the pasta cooking water. Add the butter and lemon zest and juice, and scatter over the parsley. Swirl everything together, moving it all around the pan until the butter melts and the sauce has reduced and coated the pasta. Season to taste with sea salt and plenty of freshly ground black pepper.

I love to eat this with Burrata (page 138), but if you're keeping it simple, a topping of grated Parmesan or *Pangrattato* – or both – is good too.

VEGAN OPTION
Use dried *spaghetti,* omit the butter and add an extra tablespoon of olive oil. Finish with a sprinkling of Nutritional Yeast (page 145) or *Pangrattato*.

FETTUCINE ALFREDO

Some pasta recipes are so simple it's almost funny. Beautiful ingredients make for a flavourful meal, and you can't get much simpler than pasta *Alfredo*. The cheese melts into the butter to create a rich sauce that coats the ribbons of pasta. Easy peasy.

SERVES 4

FRESH PASTA
400g/14oz egg *fettucine* (pages 22 and 33)

DRIED PASTA
360g/13oz dried *fettucine*

100g/3½oz butter, cubed

100ml/scant ½ cup pasta cooking water

80g/3oz Parmesan (vegetarian, if necessary), finely grated

Bring a large pan of water to the boil before adding salt, then cook the fettucine for 1½–2 minutes. Alternatively, if using dried pasta, follow the packet instructions.

Meanwhile, place the butter in a large saucepan over a medium heat, then use a ladle to scoop out and measure the pasta cooking water and add it to the saucepan. You don't need to be too accurate with the amount of water – you are looking to create a loose, buttery sauce.

Once the pasta is cooked, use kitchen tongs to lift it out of the pan and quickly transfer it to the sauce, gently mixing together to coat the *fettucine* well.

The next step you need to do off the heat, or the Parmesan will go stringy. Scatter over half the cheese, lifting the strands of pasta with the tongs or two tablespoons to combine and melt it. Add the remaining cheese and add more cooking water, if you need it, continuing to mix together. Season to taste with sea salt and plenty of freshly ground black pepper.

When the cheese is fully absorbed into the sauce, serve it straight away. It's nice to serve this with a fresh green salad, but it works just as well on its own.

SPAGHETTI WITH POACHED COD, CAPERS AND LEMON

I live not far from the coast near a small harbour, where I love to watch the fishing boats heading out to sea or the fishermen cleaning their vessels after a productive trip. It looks like incredibly hard work, but I'm always grateful to be able to eat such fresh, locally caught fish. There is nothing better on a warm summer's day than lightly poached cod, fragrant with lemon and garlic. The bonus here is that this is a simple and easy way to cook fish and you can't really go wrong.

SERVES 4

FRESH PASTA
400g/14oz spaghetti alla chitarra (page 37)
DRIED PASTA
360g/13oz dried spaghetti

75g/3oz butter

160ml/⅔ cup water

2 banana shallots, thinly sliced

2 garlic cloves, thinly sliced

3–4 boneless, skinless cod fillets (about 650–700g/1lb 7oz–1lb 9oz in total)

3 tablespoons capers in salt, rinsed

zest of 2 lemons; juice of ½

½ bunch of parsley (about 15g/½oz), leaves picked and chopped

Place the butter and water in a large saucepan over a low heat and stir with wooden spoon until the butter has melted. Add the shallots and garlic and cook on a medium heat for a few minutes until soft but not browned. Add the fish fillets, then cover the pan with a lid and cook for 5 minutes. Remove the lid, add the capers and lemon juice and zest, stirring them into the sauce. Gently break the fish into smaller pieces with a wooden spoon – it will fall apart quite easily. Remove from the heat while you cook the pasta.

Bring a large pan of water to the boil before adding salt, then add the spaghetti and cook for 1½–2 minutes. Alternatively, if using dried pasta, follow the packet instructions.

When the pasta is nearly ready, place the sauce back over a low heat, then use kitchen tongs to lift the pasta into the sauce. Scatter the parsley over the top and use the tongs to bring everything together. Season to taste and serve straight away with a glass of chilled white wine. If you'd like something fresh alongside, then a Rocket and Shaved Parmesan salad would be perfect (see page 144).

SPAGHETTI WITH PRAWNS, CHILLI AND GARLIC

You can use either fresh or frozen prawns (shrimp) in this dish, but if you're using frozen you need to defrost them in the fridge overnight or else remember to place them in the fridge in the morning before work. I'm trusting that you have a bottle of wine open and can use a splash in the sauce... If not, it's a good excuse to open a bottle and pour yourself a glass while you cook.

SERVES 4

FRESH PASTA
400g/14oz *spaghetti alla chitarra* (page 37)
DRIED PASTA
360g/13oz dried *spaghetti*

60ml/4 tablespoons olive oil

3 garlic cloves, finely chopped

1 whole chilli, deseeded and diced

450–500g/1lb peeled prawns (shrimp), cut into smaller pieces

50ml/3 tablespoons white wine

zest and juice of 1 lemon

150g/5½oz spinach, washed and chopped

Warm the olive oil in a large saucepan over a medium heat, then add the garlic and chilli and fry for 2 minutes until fragrant and just beginning to colour. Add the prawns, stir well and cook for 3–4 minutes. Now add the wine and reduce for 2–3 minutes. Finally, add the lemon zest and juice along with the chopped spinach, then cover with a lid for a minute or two. Take off the heat while you cook the pasta.

Bring a large pan of water to the boil before adding salt, then cook the pasta for 1½–2 minutes. Alternatively, if using dried pasta, follow the packet instructions.

Drain the *spaghetti,* reserving a ladleful of the cooking water. Transfer the pasta to the sauce and toss together, adding some of the pasta cooking water if you need to loosen the sauce a little. Season to taste with sea salt and freshly ground black pepper.

Serve straight away with Sautéed Garlicky Broccoli (see page 140).

RIGATONI WITH 'NO-VODKA SAUCE'

My friend Luigi runs a pasta factory in Brooklyn called La Trafila, where he makes several tonnes of pasta every week to sell at farmers' markets around New York. It's always nice to spend some time with him, mostly talking about pasta – flour types, machinery, popular shapes – we're both obsessed. He made me this quick vodka sauce for supper one evening, only leaving out the vodka, and I really enjoyed it. This is the version I made at home.

DRIED PASTA
360g/13oz dried *rigatoni*

30ml/2 tablespoons olive oil

2 garlic cloves, crushed

80g/3oz tomato purée (paste)

½–1 teaspoon chilli (hot pepper) flakes
(depending on how hot you like it)

250ml/1 cup double (heavy) cream

½ bunch of basil (about 15g/½oz),
leaves only

Parmesan or pecorino (vegetarian,
if necessary), grated, to finish

Heat the olive oil in a large saucepan, add the garlic and fry for a minute before adding the tomato purée and chilli flakes. Stir together and fry for 5–7 minutes until the tomato purée mixture darkens; it will start catching on the bottom of the pan, but that's what you want to capture all the flavour. Reduce the heat to low, pour in the cream and mix well – I like to use a balloon whisk. Scatter over the basil leaves, mix again and season to taste with sea salt and freshly ground black pepper. Leave to one side while you cook the pasta.

Bring a large pan of water to the boil before adding salt, then add the *rigatoni* and cook until *al dente*, following the instructions on the packet.

Drain the pasta, reserving a ladleful of the starchy cooking water, then add the pasta to the sauce. Toss or swirl together until the pasta is well coated in the sauce, adding some of the cooking water if you think it needs loosening a little.

Check the seasoning before serving with a generous topping of Parmesan or pecorino. Green Beans with Lemon (page 145) would be tasty alongside.

VEGAN OPTION
Replace the dairy cream with the same amount of oat cream. Finish the dish with Nutritional Yeast (page 145) or *Pangrattato* (page 146).

SPAGHETTI WITH CHEESY MARMITE SAUCE

'You either love it or hate it.' Marmite embraced this advertising slogan about 30 years ago, and at one point you could even buy a jar that just said 'I hate' on the side, with no mention of Marmite at all. (I suppose the brown glass jar is a giveaway, though, with its squat shape and signature yellow lid). Marmite sauce is especially good with the softer texture of fresh egg pasta, but if you love Marmite, you'll love it with either fresh or dried pasta, I promise. And if you hate it, well, give this a try. It might just surprise you.

SERVES 4

FRESH PASTA
400g/14oz spaghetti alla chitarra (page 37)

DRIED PASTA
360g/13oz dried spaghetti

2 teaspoons Marmite

80g/3oz butter, cubed

80g/3oz Parmesan (vegetarian, if necessary), finely grated, plus extra to serve

Bring a large pan of water to the boil before adding salt, then cook the spaghetti for 1½–2 minutes. Alternatively, if using dried pasta, follow the packet instructions.

Meanwhile, add half a ladleful of the pasta cooking water to a large saucepan set over a medium heat. Add the Marmite and butter, swirling the pan to melt the butter.

When the spaghetti is cooked, use kitchen tongs to transfer it to the saucepan, taking along some of the starchy cooking water, which will cling to the strands. Continue to cook the pasta in the sauce, swirling it around the pan with the tongs until the sauce thickens and starts to coat the pasta. Remove from the heat, grind over a twist or two of black pepper and scatter with the Parmesan. Continue mixing or tossing to prevent the cheese going stringy as it melts into the sauce.

Serve in warmed bowls, with extra Parmesan on top, and a Rocket and Shaved Parmesan salad (page 144) alongside, if you like.

SPAGHETTI WITH SQUID, CHILLI AND GARLIC

When on holiday in Italy, I am really drawn to eating seafood dishes, from refreshing *crudo* (dressed raw seafood) to *calamari fritti* (fried squid rings). It's a real treat. I think of the Italian coast when I make this simple squid pasta. It's especially easy to make if you buy cleaned squid at the supermarket or from your fishmonger. If you buy frozen squid, you will need to defrost it in the fridge overnight or else remember to place it in the fridge in the morning before work.

SERVES 4

FRESH PASTA
400g/14oz *spaghetti alla chitarra* (page 37)
DRIED PASTA
360g/13oz dried *spaghetti*

45ml/3 tablespoons olive oil
3 garlic cloves, finely diced
2 red chillies, deseeded and finely chopped
450g/1lb squid, sliced into finger-sized pieces
350g/12oz cherry tomatoes, halved
bunch of parsley (about 25g/1oz), leaves picked and chopped
juice of ½ lemon
Pangrattato (page 146), to serve

Heat the olive oil in a large saucepan and fry the garlic for about a minute, then add the chillies. Continue to cook on a low heat for 2–3 minutes until fragrant.

Increase the heat to medium, add the squid and cook for 3 minutes, then add the tomatoes and cook for a further 3–4 minutes. Gently break the tomatoes with the back of a wooden spoon. Keep the sauce on a very low heat while you cook the pasta.

Bring a large pan of water to the boil before adding salt, then cook the *spaghetti* for 1½–2 minutes. Alternatively, if using dried pasta, follow the packet instructions.

Lift the pasta out of the pan using kitchen tongs and add it to the sauce. Scatter over the parsley, add the lemon juice and toss everything together. You may need to add some more pasta cooking water to make sure the pasta is well coated with the sauce. Check the seasoning.

Divide between four plates and add a generous topping of *Pangrattato* (page 146) for a delicious crunch.

TAGLIARINI WITH TUNA AND CHERRY TOMATOES

This pasta takes me back to wintertime in Poland, when I was about eight or nine years old. We used to play outside after school, running around in the snow even when it was minus 12°C/10°F, sometimes even colder. When I got back home, my cheeks would be glowing red from the cold, but I'd soon forget all about it if my mum had made tuna pasta for dinner. It was only a tin of tuna with onions and pasta, but it tasted so good. My version has cherry tomatoes and herbs, but in essence it's still simple and makes for an easy-going supper.

SERVES 4

FRESH PASTA
400g/14oz egg *tagliarini* (pages 22 and 33)
DRIED PASTA
360g/13oz dried *tagliarini* or *spaghettini*

45ml/3 tablespoons olive oil

4 garlic cloves, thinly sliced

2 celery sticks, finely chopped

350g/12oz cherry tomatoes, halved

160g/5¾oz tuna, drained (I use canned tuna in olive oil)

juice of 1 lemon

½ bunch of parsley (about 15g/½oz), leaves picked and chopped

½ bunch of basil (about 15g/½oz), leaves picked and torn

Heat the oil in a large saucepan, add the garlic and fry on a medium heat for a minute or so until fragrant, then add the celery and tomatoes and cook for 10 minutes, stirring occasionally. When the tomatoes have softened and start to collapse a little, crush them with the back of a wooden spoon to release all their lovely juices. Reduce the heat, then add the tuna and lemon juice. Stir everything together and leave on a low heat.

Bring a large pan of water to the boil before adding salt, then cook the *tagliarini* for 1½–2 minutes. Alternatively, if using dried pasta, follow the packet instructions.

Drain the pasta and add it to the saucepan, reserving some of the pasta cooking water to loosen the sauce if you need to. Swirl it all together, add the herbs and season to taste with sea salt and freshly ground black pepper.

Divide between four warmed bowls and serve with a bowl of Romaine Lettuce with Avocado and Parmesan (page 144) on the side. A topping of *Pangrattato* (page 146) is always a good option, too.

PRONTO!

THIRTY MINUTES, OR THEREABOUTS

In this chapter, you'll find recipes that contain a few more ingredients, which means they may take a little longer to prepare. If your knife skills are good, you can dice a *sofrito* in no time, or if you prefer, simply use a food processor to speed up your prep. You can't always speed up the cooking time, however. Whether it's caramelizing onions, roasting aubergines (eggplant) or cooking minced (ground) beef, the flavours and textures take their own time to develop.

That doesn't mean you need to stand over the cooker the whole time – keeping an eye on things will very often do – and if you're cooking a sauce that needs to simmer for 10 minutes, then why not cook the dried pasta alongside and combine them at the end? That definitely makes dinner a bit more *pronto*.

Cooking from scratch always demands a little bit more effort. The first time you cook an unfamiliar recipe will be slower than the second and subsequent occasions; by then, the recipe is becoming an old friend and you may well have changed it to add another ingredient or two to make it your own. I hope some of these dishes will give you fresh inspiration in the kitchen. *Buon appetito!*

FETTUCINE ALLA BOLOGNESE

Bolognese doesn't have to be cooked for hours to achieve a rich depth of flavour. This recipe takes just 25 minutes to cook – not bad for a hearty lunch or supper. A food processor is handy for speeding up the prep, too.

SERVES 4

FRESH PASTA
400g/14oz egg *fettucine* (pages 22 and 33)
DRIED PASTA
360g/13oz dried *fettucine*

1 carrot, peeled and roughly chopped

2 celery sticks, roughly chopped

1 small onion, roughly chopped

2 garlic cloves, chopped

45ml/3 tablespoons olive oil

250g/9oz minced (ground) beef

250g/9oz minced (ground) pork

100ml/scant ½ cup red wine

1 x 400g/14oz tin of peeled plum tomatoes, drained

½ nutmeg, for grating

50g/2oz butter

½ bunch of parsley (about 15g/½oz), finely chopped

First prepare the vegetables that form the base of the Bolognese (this is called a *sofrito*). You can do this in a small food processor or mini chopper to save time. Place the carrot, celery, onion and garlic in the processor/chopper and blitz for 15–20 seconds until the vegetables are chopped (be careful not to end up blending them to a paste).

Heat the olive oil in a large saucepan, add the *sofrito* and fry for 5–7 minutes, stirring occasionally until the vegetables start to soften. Add the beef and pork mince, break it up a little with a wooden spoon, and cook for a further 5 minutes, or until the meat is cooked through (it will start to brown a little). Add the red wine and plum tomatoes, stir together and simmer for 10 minutes. Grate over all the nutmeg, stir in the butter and season to taste with sea salt and freshly ground black pepper.

Bring a large pan of water to the boil before adding salt, then cook the *fettucine* for 1½–2 minutes. Alternatively, if using dried pasta, follow the packet instructions.

Drain the pasta and add it to the sauce, reserving some pasta cooking water to loosen the sauce if you need to. Move the pasta around the saucepan with tongs to make sure the strands are well coated in sauce. Scatter over the parsley, check the seasoning and toss together a couple more times.

Divide between four warmed bowls and serve with Sautéed Garlicky Spinach (page 141).

VEGETARIAN OPTION
Substitute the minced meat with vegetarian mince (Quorn works well).

SPAGHETTI WITH SPINACH SAUCE

Have you ever used nutritional yeast? It has a savoury, slightly nutty flavour and adds that hint of umami to a dish. I cook with it a lot, especially when I need a substitute for cheese. It's now available in most supermarkets and a little goes a long way. My top tip: try nutritional yeast sprinkled over a dressed green salad, as it's delicious. It really encourages the kids to eat their greens. My nieces call it magic powder! You will need a blender or food processor for this recipe.

FRESH PASTA
400g/14oz *spaghetti alla chitarra* (page 37)
DRIED PASTA
360g/13oz dried *spaghetti*

250g/9oz spinach, washed

35g/1¼oz almonds

3 small garlic cloves (Confit Garlic is even better – see page 148)

25g/1oz Nutritional Yeast (page 145)

juice of 1 lemon

60ml/4 tablespoons olive oil

2 burrata, to serve (optional)

Bring a large pan of water to the boil before adding salt. Add the spinach and blanch for 1 minute, then remove with tongs and cool it straight away in a bowl of ice-cold water (this helps to keep its lovely deep green colour). Leave the pan of water to one side for cooking the pasta in when you're ready.

Place the almonds in a blender or the bowl of a food processor and blitz until they have the texture of coarse sand. Lift the spinach from the water and gently squeeze it to remove the excess moisture, then transfer it to the blender. Add the garlic, Nutritional Yeast (page 145), lemon juice and half the olive oil. Start blending, slowly pouring in the remaining olive oil while you continue to blend, until you've created a beautifully smooth, green sauce. Season to taste with sea salt and freshly ground black pepper. Transfer to a large saucepan and leave to one side while you cook the pasta.

Bring the pan of spinach water back to the boil, add the *spaghetti* and cook for 1½–2 minutes. Alternatively, if using dried pasta, follow the packet instructions.

Meanwhile, gently heat the sauce, adding half a ladleful of the pasta cooking water to loosen it slightly. When the *spaghetti* is cooked, use kitchen tongs to lift it into the sauce. Toss or stir everything together and season to taste, loosening with more pasta cooking water if needed.

Serve on four warmed plates, placing half a burrata on each plate, if you like.

VEGAN OPTION
Use dried pasta or *spaghetti alla chitarra* made with Vegan Semolina Dough (page 126) and use Nutritional Yeast (see page 145) to finish the dish.

TAGLIARINI WITH CHERRY TOMATOES AND RICOTTA SAUCE

In the summer, I sometimes take my morning cup of tea to the greenhouse, which is heady with the scent of tomatoes and basil on warm days. It's always a relaxing way to start the day, and kind of romantic. When there are plenty of ripe cherry tomatoes, I use them to make this dish, which is not only easy to prepare but also light and full of flavour.

SERVES 4

FRESH PASTA
400g/14oz egg *tagliarini* (pages 22 and 33)

DRIED PASTA
360g/13oz dried *tagliarini* or *spaghettini*

60ml/4 tablespoons olive oil

2 garlic cloves, finely chopped

500g/1lb 2oz cherry tomatoes, halved

200g/7oz ricotta (check vegetarian, if necessary)

50g/2oz Parmesan (vegetarian, if necessary), grated

½ bunch of mint (about 15g/½oz), leaves only

½ bunch of basil (about 15g/½oz), leaves only

Pangrattato (page 146) or a chunk of Parmesan, to serve

Heat the olive oil in a large saucepan, add the garlic and fry on a low heat until fragrant – a minute or two will do it – then add the tomatoes and stir together. Cook for 15–20 minutes on a medium-low heat, stirring from time to time. Remove from the heat and allow to cool for 5 minutes.

When the tomatoes have cooled down, add the ricotta and Parmesan and use a wooden spoon to combine well. Season to taste with sea salt and freshly ground black pepper.

Bring a large pan of water to the boil before adding salt, then cook the *tagliarini* for 1½–2 minutes. Alternatively, if using dried pasta, follow the packet instructions.

Meanwhile, place the sauce back on a low heat, adding half a ladleful of the pasta cooking water to loosen it a little.

Drain the pasta, reserving a jugful of the cooking water, and add the pasta to the sauce. Toss or swirl everything together until the *tagliarini* is well coated, adding more of the pasta cooking water if you need it. Check the seasoning, scatter over the mint and basil leaves and toss once again.

Divide between four warmed bowls. Serve with a chunk of Parmesan for grating, or a bowl of *Pangrattato* (page 146) for those who like a little crunch with their topping.

ORZO SALAD WITH CANNELLINI BEANS AND CAVOLO NERO

In the summertime I love to eat *alfresco* whenever it's warm enough, either in the garden or out for a picnic. Pasta salad is what's needed – something you can make ahead, pack in a container to take to the park or the beach, but that's also quick to make on the spot if hungry friends turn up. Use any short, dried pasta shape: *fusilli* or *messicani*, or *orzo*. I recommend using a jar of beans rather than canned, as they have a better texture and a fuller flavour.

SERVES 4

DRIED PASTA
280g/10oz *orzo* or other short, dried pasta

200g/7oz cavolo nero

30ml/2 tablespoons olive oil

1 medium leek, quartered lengthways
  and sliced

4 garlic cloves, thinly sliced

8 anchovy fillets

2 tablespoons capers

½ teaspoon chilli (hot pepper) flakes

500g/1lb 2oz jar of cannellini beans, drained

zest and juice of 1 lemon

1 bunch of parsley (about 25g/1oz),
  finely chopped

First, prepare the cavolo nero by stripping away the stalks, which you can then discard. Chop the leaves as you like – I prefer to cut them up quite finely – then set aside.

Heat the olive oil in a large saucepan, add the leek and garlic and fry on a medium heat for 5 minutes until the vegetables soften. Mix in the anchovies, capers and chilli flakes and cook until the anchovies fully dissolve in the oil. The kitchen will be filled with the beautiful rich fragrance of the fish.

Add the cavolo nero leaves, stir everything together and cook for a further 4–5 minutes until the leaves have softened. Remove from the heat, add the cannellini beans, lemon zest and juice, and toss together well. Transfer to a large serving bowl and set to one side.

Bring a large pan of water to the boil before adding salt, then cook the *orzo* until *al dente*, following the cooking time suggested on the packet.

Drain the pasta, add it to the bean mixture and scatter over the parsley. Mix together, then season to taste with sea salt and freshly ground black pepper.

SPAGHETTI WITH BUTTER TOMATO SAUCE

Whenever I make this pasta, I think of *The Sopranos* episode where Jackie Aprile Jr is trying to buy a handgun from Ralph Cifaretto, while Ralph is preoccupied with making his signature pasta dish, *macaroni* in butter tomato sauce. The butter here softens the sometimes sharp acidity of canned tomatoes, making this a particularly creamy tomato sauce.

SERVES 4

FRESH PASTA
400g/14oz egg *spaghetti alla chitarra* (pages 22 and 37)

DRIED PASTA
360g/13oz dried *spaghetti*

60ml/4 tablespoons olive oil

5 garlic cloves, finely chopped

2 x 400g/14oz tins of plum tomatoes or 600g/1lb 5oz fresh cherry tomatoes

1 teaspoon balsamic vinegar

60g/2oz butter, cubed

½ bunch of basil (about 15g/½oz), leaves only (optional)

grated Parmesan (vegetarian, if necessary) or pecorino, to serve

Heat the olive oil in a large saucepan on a medium heat and fry the garlic for a couple of minutes until fragrant but without letting it colour. Add the tomatoes (leave the cherry tomatoes whole if you're using fresh ones) and cook for 40 minutes on a medium-low heat, stirring occasionally. Half-cover the pan with a lid, so that the tomatoes don't splatter the stove-top as they bubble away.

At the end of the cooking time, break up the tomatoes with the back of a wooden spoon if they haven't already split. Add the balsamic vinegar, then season to taste with sea salt and freshly ground black pepper. Leave the sauce on a low heat while you cook the pasta.

Bring a large pan of water to the boil before adding the salt, then cook the *spaghetti* for 1½–2 minutes. Alternatively, if using dried pasta, follow the packet instructions.

Drain the pasta, reserving some of the cooking water, and add the pasta to the sauce. Toss everything together, then stir in the butter until it melts. If you need to loosen it slightly, add a dash of the pasta cooking water. Remove from the heat and scatter over a handful of basil leaves, if using.

Serve straight away with a generous grating of Parmesan or pecorino.

TAGLIARINI WITH BASIL AND PUMPKIN SEED PESTO

Pesto is my go-to recipe for a quick and easy dinner. In spring, I love gathering wild garlic (ramsons) to make pesto, and in the summer I'm always making big batches from the basil in the greenhouse. A supermarket basil plant will keep going for ages if you can repot it and leave it on a sunny windowsill. Supper will always be *pronto* if you have an emergency stock of pesto in the freezer, so why not double up on the recipe and freeze some for another day? You will need a food processor for this recipe.

SERVES 4

FRESH PASTA
400g/14oz egg *tagliarini* (pages 22 and 33)

DRIED PASTA
360g/13oz dried *tagliarini*

60g/2oz pumpkin seeds, toasted

large bunch of basil (about 40g/1½oz)

½ bunch of garden mint (about 15g/½oz)

juice of ½ lemon

2 garlic cloves or Confit Garlic (page 148),
   if you have it

150ml/5fl oz olive oil

grated Parmesan or Nutritional Yeast (page
   145), to serve

First, toast the pumpkin seeds in a medium saucepan for 5–6 minutes, turning from time to time until they smell nutty and begin to brown. Tip onto a plate to cool a little.

When cooled, add the seeds to the bowl of a food processor and blitz for 10 seconds or so, making sure that they're evenly ground – you're aiming for the texture of coarse sand. Add the herbs, lemon juice, garlic and half the olive oil. Continue to blend while slowly pouring the remaining olive oil through the funnel in the lid. Season to taste with salt – be generous, it can take more salt than you'd think. Use a spatula to scrape every last bit of delicious pesto into a large saucepan.

Bring a large pan of water to the boil before adding salt, then cook the *tagliarini* for 1½–2 minutes. Alternatively, if using dried pasta, follow the packet instructions.

Use tongs to lift the *tagliarini* into the pesto sauce, adding half a ladleful of the pasta cooking water to loosen it a little. Place the saucepan on a medium-low heat and combine by tossing the pasta or moving it around the pan with the tongs or spatula. Check the seasoning and add more pasta cooking water, if needed.

Divide between four shallow bowls, finishing each dish with a generous blizzard of Parmesan or a topping of Nutritional Yeast (page 145).

VEGAN OPTION
Use dried pasta and Nutritional Yeast (page 145) to finish the dish.

FETTUCINE WITH RICOTTA AND RED PEPPER SAUCE

Since I got a greenhouse, I've taken over all the space to grow tomatoes, basil and peppers; the geraniums have been evicted. I'm always impatient to see what's ready to eat. The tomatoes and basil were all harvested in the summer, but the Corno peppers really made me wait. They showed just a hint of the red skin I'd been waiting for in the very week that I was due to go on holiday. Classic. You will need a food processor for this recipe.

SERVES 4

FRESH PASTA
400g/14oz egg *fettucine* (pages 22 and 33)
DRIED PASTA
360g/13oz dried *fettucine*

30ml/2 tablespoons olive oil

2 garlic cloves, sliced

1 shallot, roughly chopped

1 tablespoon capers, rinsed

1 tablespoon tomato purée (paste)

1 red (bell) pepper (around 180g/6½oz), deseeded and sliced

pinch of salt

15ml/1 tablespoon water

200g/7oz ricotta (check vegetarian, if necessary)

juice of ½ lemon

½ bunch of parsley (about 15g/½oz), leaves picked and chopped

½ bunch of basil (about 15g/½oz), leaves only

Heat the olive oil in a medium saucepan over a medium heat. Add the garlic and shallot and fry for 5 minutes until they soften and start to turn golden. Add the capers, tomato purée, red pepper and a pinch of salt, and cook for a further 10 minutes, stirring occasionally. The tomato purée will stick to the pan slightly, but don't worry, that's part of the plan! Add the water, then use a spatula to stir everything together and capture all the flavours. Remove the pan from the heat and leave to one side to cool down a little.

When the vegetables are cool enough, transfer them to the bowl of a food processor and scoop in the ricotta. Blend until smooth, making sure there are no chunky bits left, then transfer to a large saucepan. Leave to one side while you cook the pasta.

Bring a large pan of water to the boil before adding salt, then cook the *fettucine* for 1½–2 minutes. Alternatively, if using dried pasta, follow the packet instructions.

Use tongs to transfer the *fettucine* to the sauce (it will carry some of the starchy pasta cooking water with it – just what you want). Return the sauce to a low heat and swirl everything together, so that the sauce clings to the strands of pasta. If the sauce is a little too thick, loosen it with more of the pasta cooking water. Finally, add the lemon juice and herbs and season to taste with sea salt and freshly ground black pepper.

Divide between four bowls. This is delicious served with a large bowl of Sautéed Garlicky Broccoli on the side (page 140). Enjoy.

FARFALLE WITH CHORIZO AND FIG

Since moving to London, I have usually favoured working in Italian restaurants, apart from the two years I was head chef at a Spanish restaurant called Pizarro. Besides the *Padrón* peppers and *patatas bravas* (always crowd-pleasers), one of the most popular dishes was *chorizo al vino*, which I really enjoyed cooking. This pasta sauce is inspired by it. The spicy chorizo pairs perfectly with sweet dried figs.

SERVES 4

FRESH PASTA
400g/14oz egg *farfalle* (pages 22 and 38)
DRIED PASTA
360g/13oz dried *farfalle*

45ml/3 tablespoons olive oil
2 garlic cloves, finely diced
1 medium onion, diced
pinch of salt
200g/7oz chorizo, chopped into small pieces
1 tablespoon tomato purée (paste)
1 x 400g/14oz tin of chopped tomatoes
100g/3½oz fresh or dried figs, chopped, stalks discarded
pinch of chilli (hot pepper) flakes (optional)
½ bunch of parsley (about 15g/½oz), leaves picked and chopped
grated pecorino, to serve

Heat the olive oil in a large saucepan over a medium heat. Add the onions and garlic together with a pinch of salt and cook for 5 minutes, stirring occasionally, until the onions are soft and beginning to turn golden. Add the chorizo and the tomato purée and continue to cook for 5–6 minutes. The onions will turn golden brown and the tomato purée will start to catch on the bottom of the pan, but don't worry, that's part of the plan to capture all that flavour.

Add the tomatoes, figs and chilli flakes (if using). Stir to combine everything well, lifting any tomato purée that may be stuck to the bottom of the saucepan with a wooden spoon. Bring to a simmer and cook on a medium-low heat for 10 minutes. The sauce will reduce and thicken nicely.

Meanwhile, bring a large pan of water to the boil before adding salt, then cook the *farfalle* for 2 minutes. Alternatively, if using dried pasta, follow the packet instructions.

Drain the pasta, reserving a jugful of the cooking water, and add the pasta to the sauce. Stir or swirl together, adding a splash more cooking water if you think it's needed, then scatter over the chopped parsley and check the seasoning.

Serve in four warmed bowls, finishing each bowl with grated pecorino. A bowl of Romaine Lettuce with Avocado and Parmesan (page 144) would be perfect alongside.

SPAGHETTI ALLA TAPENADE

Inspired by a beautiful tapenade that one of our friends made recently, I came up with this tapenade sauce, which pairs perfectly with pasta. I buy olives from our local farm shop. There's something so nice about scooping olives out of a large bowl into a container to take home – the next best thing to shopping in a Mediterranean market. Make sure you use good-quality olives and anchovies for this sauce as it really does lift the flavour. You will need a food processor for this recipe.

FRESH PASTA
400g/14oz *spaghetti alla chitarra* (page 37)

DRIED PASTA
360g/13oz dried *spaghetti*

90ml/6 tablespoons olive oil

200g/7oz kalamata olives, pitted

6 anchovy fillets

2 teaspoons salted capers, rinsed

zest of 1 lemon; juice of ½

2 garlic cloves, finely chopped

1 bunch of parsley (about 25g/1oz), leaves picked and finely chopped

3 tablespoons *Pangrattato* (page 146) or grated Parmesan, to serve

Place half the olive oil in the bowl of a food processor, then add the olives, anchovies, capers, and lemon zest and juice, then pulse for 10–15 seconds until the ingredients are just chopped into little pieces (you don't want a purée, but something with plenty of texture). Transfer the mixture to a small bowl.

Bring a large pan of water to the boil before adding salt, then cook the *spaghetti* for 1½–2 minutes. Alternatively, if using dried pasta, follow the packet instructions.

Meanwhile, heat the remaining olive oil in a large saucepan. Add the garlic and fry for 30 seconds.

Use tongs to lift the *spaghetti* into the garlicky oil (it will carry some of the starchy pasta cooking water with it – just what you want). Toss the pasta in the garlicky oil, then add the tapenade and parsley and swirl everything together, adding more pasta cooking water if the sauce needs to be loosened a little. Once the pasta is well coated in the sauce, season to taste with sea salt and freshly ground black pepper.

Serve straight away with plenty of Parmesan or some delicious crunchy *Pangrattato* (page 146). A bowl of Green Beans with Lemon (page 145) is good alongside. A glass of robust red wine is the perfect accompaniment, too.

VEGAN OPTION

Use dried pasta or *spaghetti alla chitarra* made with Vegan Semolina Dough (page 26).

Substitute the anchovies with 1 teaspoon of white miso and finish the dish with *Pangrattato* (page 146). or Nutritional Yeast (page 145).

CAVATELLI ALLA PRIMAVERA

I had never heard of *pasta primavera* until somebody asked me for the recipe. It turns out to be a 1970s Italian-American classic, involving some debate about who invented the dish, and which now seems to come in a bewildering number of versions, including a whole medley of vegetables and half a pint of cream. This is my version, full of spring flavour; no cream, but my ode to the joy of fresh spring vegetables. If you are not vegan, Burrata (page 138) is good alongside this dish; a glass of crisp white wine is even better.

SERVES 4

FRESH PASTA
400g/14oz vegan semolina *cavatelli* (pages 26 and 39)

DRIED PASTA
360g/13oz dried *rigatoni* or *messicani*

45ml/3 tablespoons olive oil

2 banana shallots, sliced lengthways into crescent moons

2 garlic cloves, thinly sliced

2 small courgettes (zucchini) (about 160g/5½oz), cut into matchsticks

200g/7oz asparagus, ends trimmed, chopped into half-thumb lengths

120g/4oz frozen peas (*petits pois*, if you have them)

50ml/3 tablespoons water

100g/3½oz spinach, washed

½ bunch of basil (about 15g/½oz), leaves only

½ bunch of mint (about 15g/½oz), leaves only

zest and juice of 1 lemon

Heat the olive oil in a large saucepan over a medium heat and fry the shallots and garlic for 5 minutes until they soften and start to smell sweet. Add the courgettes, asparagus, peas and water, mix with a wooden spoon and cover with a lid. Cook for 5 minutes until the vegetables are soft but retain some bite. Turn off the heat, stir in the spinach and re-cover with the lid. Leave to one side to let the spinach wilt.

Bring a large pan of water to the boil before adding salt, then cook the *cavatelli* for 2½–3 minutes. Alternatively, if using dried pasta, follow the packet instructions.

Drain the pasta, reserving a jugful of the cooking water. Place the sauce back on the heat, turning with a wooden spoon to combine the spinach with the other vegetables, then add the *cavatelli* and a generous splash of the starchy cooking water. Mix well together, then add the herbs, lemon zest and juice before seasoning to taste with sea salt and freshly ground black pepper. Stir to mix.

Transfer the pasta to a large, warmed serving bowl, place in the middle of the table and let everyone help themselves.

ORZO SALAD WITH TUNA AND MOZZARELLA

When the temperature in London hits 30°C/86°F in the summertime, it's nice to think about escaping the city, even if it's only for the weekend. Picnics and outdoor lunches are what's needed, followed by a little siesta. My Italian friend Martina told me that on the hottest days of summer her mum used to make this salad. It's light and refreshing, and the best part is that it takes just 15–20 minutes to put together. Don't let the heat keep you out of the kitchen; you still want to cook some pasta, don't you?

SERVES 4

DRIED PASTA
280g/10oz *orzo* or other short, dried pasta

30ml/2 tablespoons olive oil

2 small onions, sliced into crescent moons

300g/10½oz cherry tomatoes, halved

160g/5½oz tin of tuna in oil, drained

2 balls of mozzarella (approx. 250g/9oz), cut into cubes

zest and juice of 1 lemon

1 bunch of parsley (about 25g/1oz), leaves picked and chopped

1 bunch of basil (about 25g/1oz), leaves picked and torn

Heat the olive oil in a medium saucepan, add the onions and fry on a medium heat for 3–4 minutes. Stir in the halved tomatoes, turn the heat up a notch and cook for 4–5 minutes until they soften a little. Take off the heat and transfer to a large serving bowl.

Break the tuna into bite-sized pieces and add to the bowl along with the cubed mozzarella, and lemon zest and juice. Mix well, then cover with a dinner plate and leave to one side.

Bring a large pan of water to the boil before adding salt, then add the *orzo* and cook until *al dente*, following the instructions on the packet.

Drain the pasta and transfer it to the serving bowl. Stir everything together, season to taste with sea salt and freshly ground black pepper and scatter over the herbs. Stir again.

You're now ready to serve lunch. *Buon appetito!*

PAPPARDELLE WITH GORGONZOLA AND SPECK

When the colder weather starts and the winter coats come out, we change the menu at work to include some rich and comforting dishes. This one is particularly popular. I like to serve it alongside some fresh greens or Sautéed Garlicky Broccoli (page 140).

SERVES 4

FRESH PASTA
400g/14oz egg *pappardelle* (pages 22 and 34)

DRIED PASTA
360g/13oz dried *pappardelle*

30ml/2 tablespoons olive oil
80–100g/3–3½oz speck, thinly sliced
150g/5½oz gorgonzola dolce
180ml/¾ cup double (heavy) cream
½ head of red radicchio, shredded
juice of ½ lemon

Heat the olive oil in a large saucepan, add the speck and fry for 5 minutes on a medium heat until the meat starts to crispen around the edges. Reduce the heat, break up the gorgonzola and add it to the pan. Use a wooden spoon to mix in the cheese until it melts completely, then pour over the double cream. Stir once more, then keep the saucepan on a low heat while you cook the pasta (just keep an eye on it to make sure the cream doesn't boil).

Bring a large pan of water to the boil before adding salt, then cook the *pappardelle* for 1½–2 minutes. Alternatively, if using dried pasta, follow the packet instructions.

Drain the pasta, reserving a jugful of the cooking water in case you need to loosen the sauce.

Transfer the *pappardelle* to the saucepan, scatter over the chopped radicchio and squeeze over the lemon juice. Stir everything together (or toss if you feel comfortable with the technique – you don't want pasta all over the floor). Season to taste with sea salt and freshly ground black pepper, and add some pasta cooking water, if needed.

Serve straight away, along with some fresh greens.

TAGLIARINI WITH PEAS AND LEEK

Leeks cooked in butter are a wonderful thing. When I was little, my grandad Tadeusz used to take me to his allotment, which was about 20 minutes' walk from where we lived. He had neat rows of fruit bushes as well as potatoes, onions, cabbages and leeks. Back at home, he would braise the leeks in butter, sometimes with peas and potatoes. I love cooking with leeks now because they remind me of happy days back then pottering on the allotment.

SERVES 4

FRESH PASTA
400g/14oz egg *tagliarini* (pages 22 and 33)
DRIED PASTA
360g/13oz dried *tagliarini* or *spaghettini*

30ml/2 tablespoons olive oil

2 garlic cloves, thinly sliced

1 medium leek, sliced

70ml/5 tablespoons water

30g/1oz butter

250g/9oz frozen peas

½ bunch of mint (about 15g/½oz), leaves picked and roughly torn

½ bunch of basil (about 15g/½oz), leaves picked and torn

zest of 1 lemon; juice of ½

grated pecorino or Parmesan (or Nutritional Yeast [page 145]), to serve

Heat the olive oil in a medium saucepan over a medium heat and fry the garlic for 1 minute until fragrant. Add the leek and water, cover the pan with a lid and cook for 5 minutes. Add the butter and the peas, stir together and replace the lid. Take the pan off the heat and leave to one side while you cook the pasta.

Bring a large pan of water to the boil before adding salt, then cook the *tagliarini* for 1½–2 minutes. Alternatively, if using dried pasta, follow the packet instructions.

Return the saucepan to a medium heat. Use tongs to transfer the pasta to the sauce and swirl it all together or mix with the tongs. Scatter over the herbs, lemon zest and juice and toss together, then season to taste with sea salt and freshly ground black pepper.

Serve with a generous grating of pecorino or Parmesan, or Nutritional Yeast (page 145) if you like. A peppery Rocket and Shaved Parmesan salad (page 144) works so well with this dish if you'd like some greens alongside.

VEGAN OPTION
Use Vegan Semolina Dough (page 26) to make *spaghetti alla chitarra* (page 37), or simply use dried pasta. Replace the butter with more olive oil and finish the dish with Nutritional Yeast (page 145).

FARFALLE WITH CHILLI, BUTTER BEANS AND BROCCOLI

Broccoli and beans were both staples in our house when I was growing up, so they are ingredients that are close to my heart. Butter (lima) beans are wonderful, making a dish so creamy and delicious, and of course they're very healthy too, full of fibre and protein. These days, you can get beautiful beans in jars, and I always keep a jar or two in the cupboard ready to make an easy supper with a handful of other simple ingredients.

SERVES 4

FRESH PASTA
400g/14oz *farfalle* (page 38)
DRIED PASTA
360g/13oz dried *farfalle*

45ml/3 tablespoons olive oil

3 garlic cloves, finely chopped

1 red chilli, deseeded and finely chopped

200g/7oz broccoli, stems chopped,
  florets halved

50ml/3 tablespoons water

1 x 370g/13oz jar of butter (lima)
  beans, drained

zest of 1 lemon; juice of ½

small handful each of basil, mint and
  parsley, chopped

grated Parmesan (vegetarian, if necessary),
  to serve

Heat the olive oil in a large saucepan and fry the garlic and chilli for a couple of minutes on a medium heat until fragrant but not browned. Add the broccoli stems and cook for 5 minutes, stirring occasionally, then add the broccoli florets and water. Cover the pan with a lid and cook for a further 3–4 minutes until the broccoli is tender. Stir in the butter beans, lemon zest and juice, mixing well, then season to taste with sea salt and freshly ground black pepper. Leave the sauce on a very low heat while you cook the pasta.

Bring a large pan of water to the boil before adding salt, then cook the *farfalle* for 2 minutes. Alternatively, if using dried pasta, follow the packet instructions.

Drain the pasta, reserving a small jugful of the cooking water, then add the pasta to the pan of beans. Add a generous splash of the pasta water to loosen the sauce, scatter over the herbs and toss everything together, adding more water if necessary. Check the seasoning.

Serve with a generous grating of Parmesan and enjoy a bowl of warming comfort food.

VEGAN OPTION
Use dried *farfalle* and finish the dish with Nutritional Yeast (page 145) instead of Parmesan.

FETTUCINE WITH COURGETTE, SPINACH AND TOFU SAUCE

Every year I swear we only need one courgette (zucchini) plant in the veg patch, and every year I'm so proud of my seedlings that I end up planting them all. Courgette city is the result, so I'm always looking for ways to cook our abundant crop. Courgettes pair well with ricotta or Parmesan, but here I've used tofu for a dairy-free sauce. You will need a blender or food processor for this recipe.

FRESH PASTA
400g/14oz egg *fettucine* (pages 22 and 33)

DRIED PASTA
360g/13oz dried *fettucine*

75ml/5 tablespoons olive oil

1 medium onion, sliced into crescent moons

2 garlic cloves, finely chopped

2 small courgettes (zucchini) (around 300g/10½oz), roughly chopped

pinch of salt

150g/5½oz spinach

200g/7oz silken tofu

1 red chilli, finely diced

juice of ½ lemon

½ bunch of basil (about 15g/½oz), leaves only

Nutritional Yeast or *Pangrattato* (pages 145 and 146), to serve

Heat 45ml/3 tablespoons of the olive oil in a large saucepan and fry the onion and garlic for 5 minutes until softened but not browned. Add the courgettes along with a pinch of salt and cook for a further 5–7 minutes until the vegetables are nice and soft. Turn the heat off, add the spinach and cover the pan with a lid. After 5 minutes or so the spinach will have wilted, so take off the lid and allow to cool a little.

Add the cooked vegetables to a blender or food processor along with the silken tofu and blend to a nice, smooth sauce. Set to one side.

Set the same saucepan over a medium heat (there's no need to wash it), add the remaining 30ml/2 tablespoons of olive oil and fry the chilli for 40 seconds before reducing the heat to medium-low and adding the sauce from the blender. Mix well and keep on a low heat while you cook the pasta.

Bring a large pan of water to the boil before adding salt, then cook the *fettucine* for 1½–2 minutes. Alternatively, if using dried pasta, follow the packet instructions.

Drain the *fettucine*, reserving a jugful of the cooking water, and add the pasta to the sauce. Swirl together, adding the lemon juice and basil leaves and seasoning to taste with sea salt and freshly ground black pepper. Serve with a generous topping of Nutritional Yeast or *Pangrattato* (pages 145 and 146).

VEGAN OPTION
Use Vegan Semolina Dough (page 26) for the pasta or substitute with dried *fettucine*.

PAPPARDELLE WITH SAUSAGE AND LEEK

I've always loved sausages. When I was growing up, there was nearly always a string of smoky *wiejska* sausages in the fridge at home, neatly wrapped in greaseproof paper. For this dish you need to use really good-quality pork. Nothing else will do.

SERVES 4

FRESH PASTA
400g/14oz egg *pappardelle* (pages 22 and 34)

DRIED PASTA
360g/13oz dried *pappardelle*

1 teaspoon fennel seeds

45ml/3 tablespoons olive oil

1 onion, diced

2 garlic cloves, finely chopped

1 medium leek, sliced

pinch of salt

350–400g/12–14oz good-quality pork sausages

50ml/3 tablespoons white wine

100ml/scant ½ cup double (heavy) cream

½ bunch of parsley (about 15g/½oz), leaves picked and finely chopped

grated Parmesan, to serve

Set a large saucepan over a medium heat, add the fennel seeds and lightly toast them for 2 minutes, turning with a wooden spoon, so they toast evenly. Add the olive oil, onion, garlic, leek and a pinch of salt and cook for 5–6 minutes until the vegetables soften.

Squeeze the pork sausages out of their skins and drop them into the pan, breaking up the meat with a wooden spoon to create smaller pieces. Cook for 5–6 minutes, stirring occasionally. Pour over the white wine and reduce it for a minute or two, then pour over the double cream and mix into the sauce. Keep the saucepan on a low heat while you cook the pasta.

Bring a large pan of water to the boil before adding the salt, then cook the *pappardelle* for 1½–2 minutes. Alternatively, if using dried pasta, follow the packet instructions.

Transfer the pasta to the sauce using tongs, carrying over some of the starchy cooking water, which will cling to the strands. Increase the heat and toss the *pappardelle* or mix it with a wooden spoon until the sauce thickens and coats the pasta. Season to taste with sea salt and freshly ground black pepper, then scatter over the parsley and swirl once again.

Serve with a blizzard of Parmesan over each bowl for a warming winter supper.

CAVATELLI WITH GORGONZOLA, SPINACH AND WALNUTS

This is a rich and creamy dish. If you eat it for lunch, I suspect you may be wanting an afternoon nap. You will need a blender or food processor for this recipe.

SERVES 4

FRESH PASTA
400g/14oz vegan semolina *cavatelli* (pages 26 and 39)

DRIED PASTA
360g/13oz dried *rigatoni* or *messicani*

35g/1¼oz walnuts, roughly chopped

30ml/2 tablespoons olive oil

2 garlic cloves, chopped

2 small shallots, thinly sliced

150g/5½oz gorgonzola dolce

150ml/scant ⅔ cup double (heavy) cream

250g/9oz spinach, washed

juice of ½ lemon

Place the walnuts in a dry frying pan (skillet) over a medium heat and toast, turning occasionally, until they begin to smell fragrant and turn golden brown around the edges. This should take 4–5 minutes (keep an eye on them as you don't want them to scorch). Tip the toasted nuts into a small bowl and set aside to cool.

Heat the olive oil in a large saucepan and fry the garlic and shallots for 5 minutes on a medium heat, stirring occasionally, until they soften and have a hint of colour. Crumble the gorgonzola into the pan, then stir with a wooden spoon and allow the cheese to melt. Pour in the double cream and whisk everything together. Allow the sauce to come to a simmer, then add the spinach and let it wilt. Remove from the heat and allow to cool slightly.

Transfer the mixture to a blender or food processor and blitz until smooth, then scoop out the creamy sauce and return it to the saucepan. Leave to one side while you cook the pasta.

Bring a large pan of water to the boil before adding salt, then cook the *cavatelli* for 2½–3 minutes. Alternatively, if using dried pasta, follow the packet instructions.

Drain the pasta, reserving a jugful of the pasta cooking water, and add the pasta to the sauce. Place the pan back on the heat, add the lemon juice and combine everything well. Season to taste with sea salt and freshly ground black pepper. Make sure that the sauce is properly heated through, then transfer to a large, warmed serving bowl, scatter over the toasted walnuts, and enjoy sharing your supper together.

FETTUCINE WITH SQUASH AND MUSHROOMS

A few years ago, when I grew my first pumpkins, I didn't know much about gardening at all. I planted three Crown Prince and three Red Kuri squashes, which didn't seem like a lot. Months passed, and the plants grew and grew, sprawling right across the garden into a tangled patch of trailing stems. In the end, I harvested around 60 pumpkins, and even though I left a row of them on the garden wall for passers-by to help themselves, I still ate an awful lot of squash that winter. For this recipe, I've used a butternut squash, but feel free to choose your own favourite variety. You will need a blender or food processor for this recipe.

FRESH PASTA
400g/14oz egg *fettucine* (pages 22 and 33)
DRIED PASTA
360g/13oz dried *fettucine*

60ml/4 tablespoons olive oil

3 garlic cloves, peeled

500g/1lb 2oz butternut squash, peeled and chopped into 1cm/½in cubes

220ml/scant 1 cup water

60ml/4 tablespoons double (heavy) cream

4 tablespoons Nutritional Yeast (page 145)

240g/8½oz chestnut (cremini) mushrooms, sliced

juice of ½ lemon

1 bunch of parsley (about 25g/1oz), leaves picked and finely chopped

grated pecorino or finely chopped almonds, to serve

Heat half the olive oil in a medium saucepan, add the garlic cloves and the squash and fry for 3 minutes, stirring occasionally. Add the water, bring to the boil, then cover the pan with a lid and simmer for 6–8 minutes, or until the squash is soft. Remove from the heat and transfer to a blender or food processor, including any water left in the pan. Add the double cream and Nutritional Yeast (page 145), then blitz until smooth. Leave to one side.

Heat the remaining olive oil in a large saucepan and fry the mushrooms on a medium heat for 4–5 minutes. Reduce the heat, then add the blended pumpkin along with the lemon juice. Stir together and season to taste with sea salt and freshly ground black pepper. Leave to one side.

Bring a large pan of water to the boil before adding salt, then cook the *fettucine* for 1½–2 minutes. Alternatively, if using dried pasta, follow the packet instructions.

Place the sauce back on the heat. Drain the *fettucine*, reserving a jugful of the pasta cooking water, and transfer the pasta to the sauce. Scatter over the parsley and toss everything together, adding more cooking water if you need to loosen the sauce. Check the seasoning.

Serve with a dish of grated pecorino or chopped almonds as a topping, maybe with a glass or two of good red wine.

VEGAN OPTION
Make the *fettucine* using Vegan Semolina Dough (page 26) or use dried *fettucine*.

Substitute oat cream for the double cream, and finish with chopped almonds instead of pecorino.

ORZO WITH TRAY-BAKED AUBERGINE AND FETA

Orzo is one of my favourite pasta shapes. There's something about it that is very comforting, maybe because it's easy to serve in a bowl and eat with a spoon, a real throwback to childhood. Here, the *orzo* is boiled and then stirred into the tray of roasted vegetables. It's not exactly *pronto*, but it's very hands-off, as the oven does all the work for you.

SERVES 4

DRIED PASTA
260g/9½oz dried *orzo*

2 aubergines (eggplants) (about 600g/1lb 5oz in total), peeled and cut into 2cm/¾in cubes

1 onion, sliced into half-moons

350g/12oz cherry tomatoes

1 tablespoon dried oregano

60ml/4 tablespoons olive oil

200g/7oz feta (check vegetarian, if necessary, cut into cubes or roughly crumbled)

150g/5½oz frozen peas

1 bunch of parsley (about 25g/1oz), leaves picked and finely chopped

juice of ½ lemon

Preheat the oven to 180°C fan/400°F/gas mark 6.

Line a large roasting tin with baking parchment, then tip in the aubergines, onion, tomatoes and oregano, drizzle with the olive oil and mix together well. Use your hands to make sure the oil and herbs coat all the vegetables, spreading them evenly across the tin. Crumble or scatter the feta across the top, then place the tray in the oven and bake for 40–45 minutes.

About 10 minutes before the timer goes, bring a large pan of water to the boil before adding salt, then cook the *orzo* following the instructions on the packet.

Roughly 1 minute before the pasta is ready, drop in the frozen peas. The water will stop boiling but the pasta will still be cooking; make sure it retains some bite but isn't over-cooked. Drain the pasta and reserve a jugful of the cooking water.

Remove the roasting tin from the oven, then add the *orzo* and peas, scatter the parsley over the top and squeeze over the lemon juice. Mix everything together using a wooden spoon, splashing in some pasta cooking water if you think it's a little dry. Season generously with sea salt and freshly ground black pepper.

Place the whole roasting tin in the middle of the table and let people dive in.

TAGLIARINI WITH CARAMELIZED ONION AND CHILLI

We often bake Simon Hopkinson's mum's cheese and onion pie at home, a favourite pie made with Lancashire cheese and onions slow-cooked in butter. I really love the flavour of onions fried in butter, there's something richly indulgent about them, but you can use olive oil and they will still taste delicious.

SERVES 4

FRESH PASTA
400g/14oz egg *tagliarini* (pages 22 and 33)

DRIED PASTA
360g/13oz dried *tagliarini* or *spaghettini*

75g/2½oz butter or 45ml/3 tablespoons olive oil

2 red onions (about 300g/10½oz), sliced into crescent moons

1 white onion (about 150g/5½oz), sliced into crescent moons

3 garlic cloves, finely chopped

pinch of salt

1 tablespoon tomato purée (paste)

½ teaspoon chilli (hot pepper) flakes

40ml/scant 3 tablespoons white wine

½ bunch of parsley (about 15g/½oz), leaves picked and finely chopped

Pangrattato (page 146) and grated Parmesan, to serve

Melt the butter or oil in a large saucepan, add the sliced onions and garlic and cook on a medium-low heat for 20–25 minutes, stirring occasionally. The onions will be beautifully soft and start to smell caramelized. Add a pinch of salt along with the tomato purée and chilli flakes and cook for a further 10 minutes. Pour over the white wine to deglaze the pan – lifting any sticky, slightly caught onions from the bottom, which carry so much flavour – then leave on a very low heat while you cook the pasta.

Bring a large pan of water to the boil before adding salt, then cook the *tagliarini* for 1½–2 minutes. Alternatively, if using dried pasta, follow the packet instructions.

Use tongs to lift the pasta into the sauce along with half a ladleful of the pasta cooking water. Toss together and season to taste with sea salt and freshly ground black pepper. Scatter over the chopped parsley and toss again to mix well.

Divide between four warmed plates and top with herby *Pangrattato* (page 146) and a generous grating of Parmesan, perhaps with a bowl of Sautéed Garlicky Broccoli (page 140) to share alongside.

VEGAN OPTION
Use Vegan Semolina Dough (page 26) to make *spaghetti alla chitarra* (page 37), or simply use dried *tagliarini*. Use olive oil instead of butter to cook the onions, and serve with *Pangrattato* or Nutritional Yeast (pages 146 and 145).

PAPPARDELLE, CAVOLO NERO AND SAUSAGE

Cavolo nero always makes me think of my friend and neighbour Steve. Every summer there is some drama playing out in his vegetable garden. This year, it's the cabbage white caterpillars, which are determined to eat his greens. Apart from sharing with me his knowledge about how to grow vegetables, I often find a little basket of produce that Steve has left on the doorstep, containing the things we didn't manage to grow ourselves. Cavolo nero is a particular treat, if the caterpillars don't eat it all first. You will need a blender or food processor for this recipe.

FRESH PASTA
400g/14oz *pappardelle* (page 34)
DRIED PASTA
360g/13oz dried *pappardelle*

200g/7oz cavolo nero
60ml/4 tablespoons olive oil
75ml/5 tablespoons water
juice of 1 lemon
400g/14oz good-quality pork sausages
2 garlic cloves, thinly sliced
1 onion, diced
grated Parmesan, to serve

Remove and discard the stalks from the cavolo nero and wash the stripped leaves under cold water. Bring a large pan of water to the boil before adding salt. Blanch the leaves for 30 seconds, then immediately transfer them to a bowl of cold water (this will help the leaves to keep their colour). Set aside the pan of salted water to cook the pasta in.

Squeeze the cavolo nero leaves to remove as much of the water as you can, then place them in a blender or food processor. Add half the olive oil, along with the water and lemon juice, blitz to a smooth consistency and leave to one side.

Squeeze the sausage meat out of the skins. Heat the remaining olive oil in a large saucepan, add the garlic and onion and fry for 4–5 minutes on a medium heat until softened but not browned. Stir in the meat and fry for a further 3–4 minutes until it begins to brown a little. Use a wooden spoon to break the meat into smaller chunks. Now transfer the cavolo nero sauce to the pan along with half a ladleful of the cavolo nero cooking water. Stir together well and keep on a low heat while you cook the pasta.

Bring the pan of water back to a rolling boil, then drop in the *pappardelle* and cook for 1½–2 minutes. Alternatively, if using dried pasta, follow the packet instructions.

Lift the cooked *pappardelle* into the sauce with kitchen tongs. Increase the heat to medium, swirl the pasta and sauce together and allow the sauce to reduce a little, so it clings to the strands of pasta. Season to taste with sea salt and freshly ground black pepper.

Serve with a good scattering of Parmesan over the top of each plate.

SPAGHETTI WITH OLIVES, ANCHOVIES AND ROCKET

SERVES 4

FRESH PASTA
400g/14oz egg *spaghetti alla chitarra* (pages 22 and 37)

DRIED PASTA
360g/13oz dried *spaghetti*

45ml/3 tablespoons olive oil

3 garlic cloves, finely chopped

pinch of chilli (hot pepper) flakes, or to taste

150g/5½oz pitted olives, roughly chopped

7 anchovy fillets

juice of ½ lemon

150g/5½oz rocket (arugula)

I like to use a mixture of kalamata and green olives in this sauce; kalamata can be too strong on their own. If the olives are marinated in herbs or chilli, you might like to adjust how many chilli (hot pepper) flakes you use. This piquant pasta is good to eat with Romaine Lettuce with Avocado and Parmesan (page 144).

Heat the olive oil in a large saucepan, add the garlic and chilli, and fry for a minute until fragrant. Next add the olives and anchovies and cook for a further 5 minutes until the anchovies have completely melted into the sauce. Leave on a low heat while you cook the pasta.

Bring a large pan of water to the boil before adding salt, then cook the *spaghetti* for 1½–2 minutes. Alternatively, if using dried pasta, follow the packet instructions.

When the *spaghetti* is cooked, use tongs to transfer it to the sauce, along with half a ladleful of the pasta cooking water. Swirl it all together or mix with the tongs, then add the lemon juice and season to taste with sea salt and freshly ground black pepper. Scatter over the rocket and toss everything together until the rocket wilts, then you're ready to serve.

RIGATONI WITH CREAMY MUSHROOMS AND CRISPY CHICKPEAS

Chickpeas (garbanzo beans) and pasta make a welcome, substantial supper for hungry people, perfect after a winter outing when you want a filling meal. The extra bite from the dried pasta is perfect here. A peppery Rocket and Shaved Parmesan salad (page 144) pairs well with this, if you'd like some greens alongside.

DRIED PASTA
360g/13oz dried *rigatoni*

FOR THE CRISPY CHICKPEAS
2 garlic cloves, crushed

2 level tablespoons plain (all-purpose) flour

pinch of sea salt

1 x 400g/14oz tin of chickpeas (garbanzo beans) (drained quantity 245g/9oz)

50g/2oz butter

FOR THE SAUCE
30ml/2 tablespoons olive oil

300g/10½oz button mushrooms, brushed clean and halved

160ml/⅔ cup double (heavy) cream

pinch of salt

juice of ½ lemon

½ bunch of parsley (about 15g/½oz), chopped (optional)

grated Parmesan (vegetarian, if necessary), to finish

First, make the crispy chickpeas. Combine the garlic, flour and a good pinch of salt in a baking tray. Tip the chickpeas into a sieve (strainer), shake them well to remove as much of the liquid as you can, then add them to the tray of flour. Stir together so that all the chickpeas are coated in the garlicky flour.

Melt the butter in a large saucepan, add the chickpeas and fry them for 5–6 minutes on a medium heat, turning from time to time, so they are evenly coloured. When the chickpeas are golden and crispy, remove with a slotted spoon to drain on a plate lined with paper towel. Leave to one side.

For the sauce, add the olive oil to the same saucepan (no need to clean it, as that buttery garlic flavour is good) and set over a medium heat. Add the mushrooms, turn the heat to high and fry for 5–7 minutes until golden brown. Reduce the heat to low, stir in the cream and half the crispy chickpeas, along with a generous pinch of salt. Stir together, then leave to one side.

Bring a large pan of water to the boil before adding salt, then cook the *rigatoni* until *al dente*, following the instructions on the packet. Drain the *rigatoni*, reserving some of that beautiful starchy cooking water, and add the pasta to the sauce. Toss everything together, then place the saucepan over a low heat to reduce the sauce slightly. Season to taste with sea salt and freshly ground black pepper, adding a splash or two of pasta cooking water if needed. Squeeze over the lemon juice and scatter over the chopped parsley (if using).

Divide between four warmed plates, finishing each one with a spoonful of crispy chickpeas and a generous grating of Parmesan. A Rocket and Shaved Parmesan salad (page 144) provides a fresh peppery contrast if you'd like to serve greens alongside.

VEGAN OPTION

Fry the chickpeas in olive oil instead of butter. Replace the dairy cream with the same amount of oat cream. Finish the dish with a generous amount of Nutritional Yeast (page 145).

SPAGHETTI ALLA CHITARRA WITH NO-COOK TOMATO SAUCE

I absolutely love tomatoes. When I was growing up, a summer breakfast was often a bowl of cottage cheese and another of juicy tomatoes, cut into chunks and scattered with flakes of salt and a twist of black pepper, served with a loaf of crusty bread. Delicious. This pasta dish is inspired by the flavour of sun-ripened tomatoes; really refreshing, with sweet and slightly sour juices and plenty of fragrant mint and basil.

SERVES 4

FRESH PASTA
400g/14oz egg *spaghetti alla chitarra* (pages 22 and 37)

DRIED PASTA
360g/13oz dried *spaghetti*

600–650g/1lb 5oz–1lb 7oz tomatoes, a mixture of varieties

½ teaspoon salt

½ teaspoon caster (granulated) sugar

zest and juice of 1 lemon

45ml/3 tablespoons olive oil

¼ teaspoon chilli (hot pepper) flakes (optional)

½ bunch of basil (about 15g/½oz), leaves picked and torn

½ bunch of mint (about 15g/½oz), leaves picked and chopped

Parmesan (vegetarian, if necessary), to serve

Roughly chop the tomatoes into small, chunky pieces and transfer to a large bowl, making sure you scoop all the juices from the cutting board into the bowl. Sprinkle with the salt, sugar and lemon zest and drizzle over the olive oil and lemon juice. Stir together with a wooden spoon, mashing the tomatoes with the back of the spoon. Cover the bowl with a plate and leave to one side for 30 minutes, so that the juice has time to run from the tomatoes.

Bring a large pan of water to the boil before adding salt, then cook the *spaghetti* for 1½–2 minutes. Alternatively, if using dried pasta, follow the packet instructions.

When the pasta is cooked, use tongs to transfer it to the bowl of tomatoes. Add the chilli flakes (if using) along with the basil and mint, and toss everything together. Season to taste with sea salt and freshly ground black pepper.

Serve with a chunk of Parmesan on the side to grate over the top.

VEGAN OPTION
Serve with a topping of *Pangrattato* (page 146) or Nutritional Yeast (page 145) instead of the Parmesan.

CAVATELLI WITH VODKA SAUSAGE RAGÙ

SERVES 4

FRESH PASTA
400g/14oz vegan semolina *cavatelli* (pages 26 and 39)

DRIED PASTA
360g/13oz dried *rigatoni* or *messicani*

45ml/3 tablespoons olive oil

2 small shallots, finely chopped

2 garlic cloves, finely chopped

300g/10½oz good-quality fennel pork sausages

90g/3¼oz tomato purée (paste)

½ teaspoon chilli (hot pepper) flakes

50ml/3 tablespoons vodka

200ml/scant 1 cup double (heavy) cream

½ bunch of basil (about 15g/½oz), leaves picked and roughly torn

grated Parmesan, to serve

I love to make vodka sauce and it's always incredibly popular; it's a beautiful, creamy sauce with a hint of spice. This version includes fennel pork sausage – track down a really good-quality sausage, preferably from the butcher.

Heat the olive oil in a large saucepan and fry the shallots and garlic for about 5 minutes until soft and golden. Squeeze the sausage meat out of the skins. Add it to the pan and fry for 4–5 minutes, stirring occasionally, using a wooden spoon to break the meat into smaller chunks. Add the tomato purée and chilli flakes, stir in well and cook for a further 5 minutes. The tomato purée will darken and start sticking to the pan, but don't worry, this is all about creating flavour. Reduce the heat, add the vodka and cook until the liquid has nearly vanished. Finally, pour over the double cream, stir together and bring to a low simmer.

Bring a large pan of water to the boil before adding salt, then cook the *cavatelli* for 1½–2 minutes. Alternatively, if using dried pasta, follow the packet instructions.

Drain the *cavatelli*, reserving a jugful of the pasta cooking water, and add the pasta to the vodka sauce. Scatter over the torn basil leaves, stir everything together and add more cooking water if the sauce needs to be loosened slightly. Season to taste with sea salt and freshly ground black pepper.

Serve straight away with grated Parmesan on top.

VEGETARIAN OPTION
When I cook this at home, I make it with veggie sausages instead. Just use your favourite vegetarian brand and chop into chunks. Check that the Parmesan is vegetarian, too.

RIGATONI WITH CANNELLINI BEANS AND ROASTED PEPPERS

It's so useful to have a jar or two of preserved vegetables in the storecupboard to add a summer flavour to a winter dish. If you can get them, cannellini beans from a jar are extra special, but a can will do just as well. Roasted peppers preserved in oil are sold in most supermarkets and are good to add to toasted sandwiches as well as to this *rigatoni* pasta sauce.

SERVES 4

DRIED PASTA

360g/13oz dried *rigatoni*

40g/1½oz butter

2 onions, sliced into crescent moons

2 garlic cloves, thinly sliced

300g/10½oz cannellini beans, from a jar
  or a can

150g/5½oz roasted peppers, from a jar

zest of 1 lemon; juice of ½

½ bunch of parsley (about 15g/½oz), chopped

Pangrattato (page 146) and/or grated
  Parmesan, to serve

Melt the butter in a large saucepan over a medium heat, then add the onions and garlic and stir together to make sure everything is nicely coated in the butter. Cook for 6 minutes until the onions are cooked but still retain some bite. If you prefer onions with a softer texture, cook for a further 5 minutes.

Drain the cannellini beans. There's no need to rinse them, just add them straight to the pan and stir together with the onions. Keep cooking over a medium heat. The beans will start to break up a little, creating a lovely sauce.

Drain the roasted peppers, discarding the oil or saving it for another dish. Roughly chop the peppers and add to the sauce along with the lemon zest and juice. Mix together, then leave to one side while you cook the pasta.

Bring a large pan of water to the boil before adding salt, then cook the *rigatoni* until *al dente*, following the instructions on the packet.

Just before the *rigatoni* is cooked, return the sauce to a low heat and stir in half a ladleful of the starchy pasta cooking water.

Drain the *rigatoni*, reserving a jugful of the cooking water in case the sauce needs to be loosened further, then add the pasta to the saucepan. Scatter over the parsley, then toss or stir everything together. Season to taste with sea salt and freshly ground black pepper.

Divide between four warmed bowls. Finish each bowl with a topping of *Pangrattato* (page 146) or Parmesan, or both, if you like.

VEGAN OPTION

Replace the butter with olive oil and use *Pangrattato* (see page 146) to finish.

TAGLIARINI ALLA PUTTANESCA

People always say how easy it is to fall in love with Naples. It's such a busy, vibrant, noisy city and the old Spanish quarter is a maze of tiny streets slung over with washing lines, caged songbirds hanging overhead and boys on mopeds zooming over the cobbles below. *Puttanesca* is a famous Neopolitan pasta sauce. I enjoyed a wonderful *spaghetti alla puttanesca* in the tiniest café that was ready to shut for their afternoon siesta, but still welcomed us in for a late lunch.

SERVES 4

FRESH PASTA
400g/14oz egg *tagliarini* (pages 22 and 33)

DRIED PASTA
360g/13oz dried *tagliarini*

45ml/3 tablespoons olive oil

3 garlic cloves, finely chopped

½ teaspoon chilli (hot pepper) flakes

6 anchovy fillets

1 tablespoon capers

1 teaspoon tomato purée (paste)

1 x 400g/14oz tin of chopped tomatoes

50g/2oz kalamata olives, halved

½ bunch of basil (about 15g/½oz), leaves picked and torn

2 burrata, or grated Parmesan, to serve

Heat the olive oil in a large saucepan and fry the garlic and chilli flakes for a couple of minutes until fragrant. Add the anchovies and capers and continue to cook until the anchovies completely melt into the garlicky oil, then add the tomato purée. Continue to cook on a medium-low heat for 5 minutes, stirring occasionally. Add the tomatoes and olives, stir everything together and simmer for 10 minutes. The sauce will have thickened nicely and have a beautiful, rich flavour. Keep on a very low heat.

Bring a large pan of water to the boil before adding salt, then cook the *tagliarini* for 1½–2 minutes. Alternatively, if using dried pasta, follow the packet instructions.

When the pasta is cooked, add it to the sauce using kitchen tongs, which will carry over some of the starchy cooking water. Toss everything together, add the basil and a splash more pasta water if you need to loosen the sauce. Check the seasoning, adding sea salt and freshly ground black pepper to taste.

Serve straight away with either half a creamy burrata on the top, or with a generous amount of grated Parmesan.

PASTA E CECI

Pasta, chickpeas (garbanzo beans), Parmesan; these words suggest a warming bowl of soup for a chilly evening. You can make the traditional, slow-cooked version, soaking the chickpeas overnight and simmering them for an hour or two the next day, but here we want a speedy supper, so I've used canned chickpeas instead.

SERVES 4

DRIED PASTA

200g/7oz dried *orzo* (or *ditalini* or short *macaroni*)

2 garlic cloves, thinly sliced

1 medium onion, finely chopped

3 celery sticks, trimmed and sliced

2 carrots, diced

45ml/3 tablespoons olive oil

1 bay leaf

1 sprig of rosemary

1 litre/4 cups vegetable or chicken stock

piece of Parmesan rind (optional; vegetarian, if necessary)

1 x 400g/14oz tin of chickpeas (garbanzo beans), drained

grated Parmesan or pecorino, to serve

First, make the *sofrito*, the mixture that is the start of all good soups. For speed, I like to use a food processor or mini chopper, but you can dice the vegetables by hand if you don't have either of these. Otherwise, add the roughly chopped garlic, onion, celery and carrots to the bowl of a food processor and pulse a few times until they are finely chopped.

Heat the olive oil in a medium pan, add the *sofrito* and cook on a medium heat for 5 minutes. Add the herbs and cook for a further 7–10 minutes until the vegetables are soft and fragrant.

Pour the stock into the pan and add the Parmesan rind if you happen to have one kicking around the freezer. Bring to a simmer and cook for 15 minutes.

Remove the rind and herbs from the broth (the rosemary will have broken up, so you may need to fish around for the leaves – they can be a little sharp to eat). Add the chickpeas and dried pasta to the pan and bring back to a good simmer. Cook until the pasta is *al dente* (follow the instructions on the packet for the recommended cooking time).

Season to taste with sea salt and freshly ground black pepper before serving in four warmed bowls, with some more Parmesan on top if you like.

VEGAN OPTION

Use vegetable stock and omit the Parmesan rind. Once the pasta is *al dente*, stir in 2 tablespoons of Nutritional Yeast (page 145).

FETTUCINI WITH CHESTNUT MUSHROOMS AND MISO

I was once given a jar of rich, flavourful homemade miso by the friend of a friend; she'd lived in Japan and was hugely knowledgeable about Japanese cuisine. That was one of the best jars of miso I ever tasted. My favourite way to eat it is with mushrooms; miso adds a salty, umami flavour to the mushrooms, making them taste extra complex and delicious. This is quick and easy comfort food – pasta, mushrooms, miso and egg, topped off with extra Parmesan cheese. Yes chef!

FRESH PASTA
400g/14oz egg *fettucine* (pages 22 and 33)
DRIED PASTA
360g/13oz dried *fettucine or tagliatelle*

60ml/4 tablespoons olive oil

300g/10½oz chestnut (cremini)
   mushrooms, sliced

2 tablespoons white miso

3 egg yolks

70g/2½oz Parmesan (vegetarian, if
   necessary), finely grated, plus extra to serve

3 garlic cloves, finely chopped

1 small bunch of parsley (about 20g/¾oz),
   leaves picked and finely chopped

Heat the olive oil in a large saucepan and fry the mushrooms on a high heat for 3–4 minutes, stirring occasionally, until golden brown. Don't overcook – the mushrooms need to stay nice and moist, and you don't want all the juices to run out. Remove from the heat and set to one side.

Add the miso, egg yolks and Parmesan to a small bowl and use a wooden spoon to combine them until you have a thick paste. Add a generous amount of black pepper and stir it in well.

Bring a large pan of water to the boil before adding salt, then cook the *fettucine* for 1½–2 minutes. Alternatively, if using dried pasta, follow the packet instructions.

Meanwhile, set the saucepan with the mushrooms back onto a medium heat, add the garlic and stir together.

When the pasta is cooked, use kitchen tongs to lift into the saucepan, carrying some of the starchy cooking water with it. Now add half a ladleful of the pasta cooking water to the miso-egg paste and quickly whisk it to combine (be speedy – you don't want to scramble the egg).

Remove the pasta from the heat and pour the miso-egg mix into the pan. Add another splash of pasta cooking water to loosen the sauce and work very quickly: toss everything together or use kitchen tongs to combine well. Season to taste with sea salt and freshly ground black pepper, then scatter the parsley over and toss once again.

Serve in four warmed bowls, with extra Parmesan for those that want it. It's good to serve with a dressed green salad alongside to balance the rich flavours of the dish.

NOT SO
PRONTO

RECIPES FOR SLOWER DAYS

For me, weekends provide time to play in the kitchen a little bit. I'm lucky, as Saturday shopping at our local market is always such a pleasure. I might come home with a bag of locally grown spinach or some new-season potatoes, a tub of crab from the fishmonger's van, or a beautiful hunk of Parmesan from Mercato Italiano. Buying fresh ingredients makes me look forward to an afternoon in the kitchen.

I find making fresh pasta very relaxing and mindful. Turning flour and eggs into beautiful golden dough still feels like magic, no matter how often I make it. If you've never made a filled pasta before, *ravioli* is a very simple shape to start with. There's nothing complicated about folding, filling and cutting the fresh dough into neat, plump parcels, but if you're just learning how to make fresh pasta, or you need enough *ravioli* to feed a crowd, then it's not something to embark on midweek, when hungry people are impatient for dinner.

All the dishes here are easy to prepare, whether they're made using fresh or dried pasta. It may be that the meat needs to be slow-cooked for flavour, that the pasta is baked in the oven for a couple of hours, or that there are a few more steps involved – a dough, a filling and a sauce for your *ravioli*, for example. Save these recipes for slower days. Put your apron on, turn up the music and start rolling your dough.

RAVIOLI WITH CRAB, MASCARPONE, CHILLI AND LEMON

This is a recipe to save for a special occasion. Crab is quite a delicate meat, so it shouldn't be overpowered with strong flavours. Combined with mascarpone, this makes a light, lemony filling with a hint of chilli, a delicious summer supper. Serve with either a fresh green salad or Sautéed Garlicky Spinach (page 141) and a glass of crisp white wine, if you like.

SERVES 4

FRESH PASTA

400g/14oz Rich Egg Dough (page 22)

FOR THE FILLING

250g/9oz white crab meat

2 red chillies, deseeded and finely diced

120g/4oz mascarpone

zest of 2 lemons; juice of 1

FOR THE SAUCE

75g/2½oz butter

75ml/5 tablespoons water

juice of ½ lemon

½ bunch of parsley (about 15g/½oz), leaves picked and chopped

Follow the instructions for making the Rich Egg Dough on page 22 and place in the fridge to rest.

Pick over the crab meat with your fingers to make sure any tiny pieces of shell are removed. Transfer to a medium bowl along with the rest of the filling ingredients and mix with a wooden spoon to combine. Season to taste with sea salt and freshly ground black pepper, then leave the bowl in the fridge until ready to use.

Now roll, fill and shape your *ravioli,* according to the instructions on page 40.

Bring a large pan of water to the boil before adding salt, then carefully add the *ravioli* and cook for 1½–2 minutes.

Meanwhile, make the sauce. Place the butter and water in a large saucepan and set it on a medium heat. As the butter melts, mix it with the water to create a light sauce, then stir in the lemon juice.

Transfer the *ravioli* to the sauce using a slotted spoon, moving them gently around the pan to make sure they are all well covered. Scatter over the chopped parsley, season to taste with sea salt and freshly ground black pepper, swirl one more time and serve straight away.

RAVIOLI WITH SPINACH AND MASCARPONE

I was once making *ravioli* for a friend who told me they weren't so keen on ricotta, so I quickly improvised and used mascarpone instead. It turned out to make a lighter filling, somehow allowing the spinach to take centre stage; never a bad thing, as I'm a big fan of spinach (one of my kitchen catchphrases is 'eat your greens').

SERVES 4

FRESH PASTA
400g/14oz Rich Egg Dough (page 22)

FOR THE FILLING
500g/1lb 2oz spinach

200g/7oz mascarpone

½ nutmeg, grated (or to taste)

zest of 2 lemons

60g/2oz Parmesan (vegetarian, if necessary), finely grated, plus extra to serve

FOR THE SAUCE
75ml/5 tablespoons water

75g/2½oz butter, chopped into small cubes

a few sage leaves

Follow the instructions for making the Rich Egg Dough on page 22 and place in the fridge to rest.

To make the filling, bring a medium pan of water to the boil before adding a generous pinch of salt. Blanch the spinach for 30 seconds, then drain it and transfer to a bowl of ice-cold water (this will help keep the fresh green colour). Drain the spinach again, squeezing as much moisture as you can from the leaves, then finely chop it and transfer to a large bowl.

Add the mascarpone, nutmeg, lemon zest and Parmesan to the bowl with the spinach and combine with a wooden spoon. Season with sea salt and freshly ground black pepper – be generous; the filling should be seasoned well. Leave the bowl in the fridge until you are ready to shape the *ravioli* (the filling will firm up slightly, which is what you want).

Now roll, fill and shape your *ravioli*, according to the instructions on page 40.

Bring a large pan of water to the boil before adding salt. Cook the ravioli, a few at a time, for around 2 minutes.

Meanwhile, to make the sauce, set a large saucepan on a medium heat, add the water and butter and swirl together to create a sauce. Use a slotted spoon to transfer the cooked *ravioli* to the sauce, moving them gently around the pan to make sure they are all well covered in the buttery emulsion. Scatter over the sage leaves and season to taste with sea salt and freshly ground black pepper. Allow the sauce to reduce and thicken a little.

Divide between four plates. I like to serve this with a chunk of Parmesan and provide the cheese grater at the table, so people can help themselves.

PAPPARDELLE SHORT RIB RAGÙ

This recipe is obviously not so *pronto*, but I love a good ragù and this just had to go in the book. Since the meat is slow-cooked, save this for a day when you're at home and up to other things – doing a jigsaw, the laundry, catching up with your favourite TV show – once the meat is in the oven, your time is your own.

This quantity makes twice as much ragù as you will need (unless you plan to feed eight hungry people). Freeze half the ragù and then you will have a supper ready for another time.

I like to add bone marrow for extra flavour, but it's tasty even if you leave this out.

SERVES 4

FRESH PASTA
400g/14oz egg *pappardelle* (pages 22
and 34)

DRIED PASTA
360g/13oz dried *pappardelle*

1.4kg/3lb 2oz short-rib beef, divided into
  smaller pieces

45ml/3 tablespoons vegetable oil

2 small onions, diced

2 carrots, diced

4 celery sticks, diced

3 garlic cloves, thinly sliced

2 bay leaves

pinch of salt

1 tablespoon tomato purée (paste)

3 pieces of bone marrow (optional)

1 x 400g/14oz tin of peeled plum tomatoes

250ml/1 cup red wine

1.2 litres/4¾ cups stock or water

grated Parmesan, to serve

Season the pieces of short rib with sea salt and freshly ground black pepper. Heat the oil in a frying pan (skillet) on a medium heat and gently brown the meat on all sides. This will take 3–4 minutes on each side. Transfer the meat to a clean casserole dish (Dutch oven) or a heavy-based roasting tin that can be used on the stove-top and set aside.

Preheat the oven to 150°C fan/325°F/gas mark 3.

To the same oil in the pan, add the vegetables and bay leaves and cook for 10 minutes over a medium heat, stirring occasionally. Add a pinch of salt with the tomato purée and cook for a further 10 minutes. Transfer the vegetables to the casserole dish or tray, along with the bone marrow (if using), plum tomatoes and red wine. Pour in enough stock to cover the meat completely and set over a medium heat until it reaches a steady simmer.

Put the lid on the casserole dish (or wrap it with kitchen foil) and place it in the oven for 4 hours, or until the meat is very tender and falling off the bone. Remove from the oven and allow to cool.

When the meat is cool enough to handle, lift it out and pick the meat off the bones (the bones can be discarded). Break up the meat a little and return it to the casserole. If you included bone marrow, extract the bones but scrape the marrow fat back into the casserole. Stir everything together and season to taste with sea salt and freshly ground black pepper.

Divide the ragù into two portions. Place half to one side to cool completely before freezing it for another day. Leave the remaining portion in the casserole dish and set over a medium heat.

Bring a large pan of water to the boil before adding salt, then add the *pappardelle* and cook for 1½–2 minutes. Alternatively, if using dried pasta, follow the packet instructions.

Use tongs to lift the *pappardelle* into the ragù, along with half a ladleful of pasta cooking water. Combine everything well and check the seasoning once more. Serve in warmed bowls and finish with a topping of grated Parmesan.

RAVIOLI WITH POTATO AND COURGETTE

Who doesn't like potatoes? They're so versatile, I can't think of a way I don't like to eat them. It may seem odd to cook potatoes with pasta, but they are actually good friends, especially if you make little pillows of *ravioli* filled with potato and courgettes (zucchini), a filling that is light and incredibly tasty. A simple herby butter sauce is the perfect way to round off the dish. Serve with a dish of Sautéed Garlicky Spinach (page 141).

SERVES 4

FRESH PASTA
400g/14oz Rich Egg Dough (page 22)

FOR THE FILLING
2 small courgettes (zucchini), approx. 220g/8oz

280g/10oz potatoes, peeled

15ml/1 tablespoon olive oil

2 garlic cloves, crushed

120ml/½ cup water

70g/2½oz Parmesan (vegetarian, if necessary), finely grated, plus extra to serve

½ bunch of mint (about 15g/½oz), leaves picked and finely chopped

½ bunch of basil (about 15g/½oz), leaves picked and finely chopped

FOR THE SAUCE
75g/2½oz butter

75ml/5 tablespoons water

½ bunch of parsley (about 15g/½oz), leaves picked and chopped

Follow the instructions for making the Rich Egg Dough on page 22 and place in the fridge to rest.

Prepare the vegetables for the filling. Quarter the courgettes lengthways and cut into 1.5cm/½ in slices. Cut the peeled potatoes into similar-sized cubes.

Heat the olive oil in a medium saucepan, add the garlic and fry for a minute or so until fragrant. Add the potatoes, courgettes and the measured water. Stir together, cover the pan with a lid and cook for 8–10 minutes until the potatoes are cooked through. Drain any remaining liquid. Mash the vegetables until smooth. I like to use a ricer as it produces such a smooth result, but if you use a standard potato masher, just make sure the mash is as smooth as possible. Place the mixture in a bowl and allow it to cool a little, then add the Parmesan, mint and basil, combining well. Season to taste with sea salt and freshly ground black pepper. Transfer to the fridge until you are ready to shape the *ravioli*.

Now roll, fill and shape your *ravioli*, according to the instructions on page 40.

Bring a large pan of water to the boil before adding salt. Cook the *ravioli*, a few at a time if you prefer, for 1½–2 minutes.

Meanwhile, make the sauce. Add the butter and water to a large saucepan over a medium heat. The butter will melt into the water to create a light butter emulsion.

When the *ravioli* are cooked, transfer them to the sauce using a slotted spoon. Move them gently around the pan to make sure they are all well covered with sauce. Check the seasoning, scatter over the parsley and swirl together once again.

Divide between four plates, scatter over more Parmesan if you like, and serve.

RAVIOLI WITH POTATO AND GOATS' CHEESE IN PESTO SAUCE

One of my earliest food memories is watching my grandad peeling potatoes to make mash while we played chess together. He never let me win, as he really wanted to force me to focus and think – a good lesson in life. Potatoes were a big thing in our Polish household in the early nineties, they came in many shapes and forms. Here, potatoes are mashed with goat's cheese as a filling for *ravioli*. Serve with basil pesto sauce and you have a perfect combination of flavours.

SERVES 4

FRESH PASTA
400g/14oz Rich Egg Dough (page 22)

FOR THE FILLING
550g/1lb 3½oz potatoes, peeled and chopped into even pieces

1 bunch of parsley (about 25g/1oz), leaves picked and chopped (keep the stalks)

140g/4½oz goats' cheese, crumbled or sliced into small pieces

1 small bunch of dill (about 20g/¾oz), picked and chopped

FOR THE PESTO SAUCE
30g/1oz pumpkin or sunflower seeds, toasted

juice of ½ lemon

1 bunch of basil (about 25g/1oz), leaves only

100–130ml/scant ½–generous ½ cup olive oil

Parmesan (vegetarian, if necessary), to serve

Follow the instructions for making the Rich Egg Dough on page 22 and place in the fridge to rest.

Place the potatoes and parsley stalks in a medium pan filled with generously salted cold water and bring to the boil. Cook the potatoes until they are soft to the point of a knife and ready to be mashed, around 15–20 minutes. Drain, discarding the parsley stalks, then mash the potatoes in a bowl (use a ricer, if you have one). Add the goats' cheese while the potato is still warm and mix well. Leave to cool down a little before adding the remaining chopped herbs, then season to taste with sea salt and freshly ground black pepper. Leave to one side while you shape the pasta.

Now roll, fill and shape your *ravioli*, according to the instructions on page 40.

Next, make the pesto. Don't forget to toast the seeds; you can do this by turning them in a frying pan (skillet) for 5–6 minutes over a medium heat. Allow to cool slightly, then use a pestle and mortar or a mini chopper to grind the seeds to the texture of coarse sand. Add the lemon juice and basil leaves and blend together, slowly pouring in the olive oil as you go. Season to taste and transfer the pesto to a large saucepan.

Bring a large pan of water to the boil before adding salt, then cook the *ravioli* for 2 minutes.

Meanwhile, place the pesto on a low heat, adding half a ladleful of pasta cooking water to loosen it. When the *ravioli* are cooked (they will bob to the surface of the pan), carefully lift them out with a slotted spoon and add them to the pesto. Swirl gently together to make sure they are all coated in the herby sauce.

Serve with a chunk of Parmesan cheese and the grater, so people can help themselves.

SPAGHETTI BAKE

I arrived home late one day to the welcoming fragrance of sweet onions and cheese. It turned out there was a pasta bake in the oven, which my partner had made using a recipe from a seventies cookbook by Rose Elliot, a pioneer of vegetarian cookery. I had never seen the book before; it had a purple cover with a smiling bean cartoon on the front – very retro – and the recipe was made with wholemeal pasta, Cheddar and canned tomatoes. I may have raised an eyebrow, but it tasted so, so good – I should think I ate at least half the dishful. This recipe is my version with the addition of garlic, mozzarella and herbs, but it's cooked the same way, in a very low oven for a couple of hours. Easy prep and two hours of free time before dinner. Dreamy.

SERVES 4

DRIED PASTA
170g/6oz dried wholemeal *spaghetti*

50g/2oz butter

4 onions, sliced into crescent moons

3 garlic cloves, thinly sliced

1 teaspoon dried oregano

2 x 400g/14oz tins of chopped tomatoes

4 sprigs of mint, leaves picked and shredded

125g/4oz mozzarella, cubed (block mozzarella is good, then freeze the rest)

½ teaspoon table salt

75g/2½oz Cheddar, coarsely grated

Melt the butter in a large saucepan over a medium heat, add the onions and garlic and cook for 10 minutes until soft, stirring from time to time. Add a generous pinch of salt, a few twists of black pepper and the oregano, stir together and cook for a further minute. Remove from the heat and set aside.

Meanwhile, tip the tomatoes into a bowl, add the mint, mozzarella cubes and salt, and combine well.

Preheat the oven to 130°C fan/300°F/gas mark 2.

Spread the onions evenly across the bottom of a baking dish (mine is around 28 x 23 x 6cm/11 x 9 x 2½in). Break the strands of *spaghetti* in half (trust me on this) and spread them over the top of the onions – it will look like you're about to play pick-up sticks – then pour the tomato sauce over the top. Poke any stray pasta strands under the sauce (or they won't cook properly) and scatter over the grated Cheddar.

Cover the dish with kitchen foil and bake in the oven for 2 hours. When the time is up, remove the bake from the oven and let it stand for 5 minutes. Remove the foil and serve with Sautéed Garlicky Broccoli (page 140) or Sautéed Garlicky Spinach (page 141). A glass of red wine would be very welcome, too.

BURRATA, GREENS AND MORE

SIDES AND EXTRAS

As anyone who has regularly watched my social media videos will know, I often finish a pasta dish with half a creamy burrata. It's more than a visual trick for the camera, as I love the way a burrata will collapse into a sauce, softening its flavour. I sometimes eat burrata instead of Parmesan – one or the other is enough to finish a dish.

In Italy, it's traditional to serve salad or greens after the pasta and meat courses, which is said to aid digestion. I suspect it's old-school these days, as not everyone will be eating a long meal of several courses, certainly not during the week. At home, I like to serve greens as a side dish, especially if the pasta has a rich or creamy sauce, but also simply because I love to eat my greens. A spoonful or two of garlicky spinach or broccoli, or a salad with a sharp dressing, helps to balance the textures and flavours in a meal.

These side dishes are all easy to put together and enough to serve four.

BURRATA TWO WAYS

This is not an everyday sort of cheese, but topping a pasta dish with half a creamy burrata is a treat; it can really make a simple meal special. Burrata is made from mozzarella and cream, so it pairs well with tomato, pesto, spinach and pumpkin sauces.

At work, I often use a vegan burrata made from soya and coconut oil, known as burella, which is made by Julienne Bruno. It's not widely available yet, but keep your eye out for it, as it's a delicious substitute for the dairy version.

Sometimes I go the extra mile and make a topping for the burrata. Here are a couple of my favourite additions.

SERVES 4

WITH CHILLI AND LEMON

2 burrata, halved

45ml/3 tablespoons olive oil

1 garlic clove, finely chopped

2 red chillies, deseeded and diced

zest of 1 lemon; juice of ½

WITH FRIED TOMATOES, BASIL AND BALSAMIC VINEGAR

2 burrata, halved

45ml/3 tablespoons olive oil

200g/7oz cherry tomatoes, halved

pinch of sea salt flakes

15ml/1 tablespoon balsamic vinegar (moscatel is also good)

handful of basil leaves, torn

WITH CHILLI AND LEMON

Tear each burrata in half with your fingers and arrange them on a serving plate. You can split them into several pieces, if you like – a rustic look is good here.

Heat the olive oil in a small saucepan over a medium heat, add the garlic and chillies and fry for 1–2 minutes until the chillies start to sizzle. Remove from the heat, quickly add the lemon zest and juice, then spoon the mixture over the burrata. Sprinkle with sea salt flakes and a few twists of black pepper.

WITH FRIED TOMATOES, BASIL AND BALSAMIC VINEGAR

Tear each burrata into halves or quarters with your fingers and arrange them on a serving plate.

Heat the olive oil in a small saucepan over a medium–high heat. When it is hot enough, add the tomatoes along with a pinch of sea salt flakes, stir together and fry for 4–5 minutes. Remove the pan from the heat, then add the vinegar and basil leaves. Use a wooden spoon to crush the tomatoes, combining all those lovely flavours together.

Spoon the tomatoes over the plate of burrata, then sprinkle over a few more flakes of sea salt and a twist of black pepper.

SAUTÉED GARLICKY BROCCOLI

This method of cooking broccoli ensures it retains its bright green colour with a nice amount of bite. It's one of my favourite greens and can be served with so many pasta dishes.

SERVES 4

1 large or 2 small heads of broccoli
45ml/3 tablespoons olive oil
2 garlic cloves, crushed
100ml/scant ½ cup boiling water

First, prepare the broccoli. Cut off the main stem, peel away any rough parts from the remaining short stems and slice into bite-sized pieces. Trim the florets.

Heat the olive oil in a large saucepan that has a lid over a medium heat, add the garlic and fry for 20 seconds before adding the broccoli, then fry for 1 minute on a high heat until the edges of the broccoli catch and start to turn golden brown.

Now – quick situation – add the boiling water to the pan and immediately cover it with the lid. Reduce the heat to medium and cook for 3 minutes until the water has just about disappeared. Remove the lid, then season to taste with sea salt and freshly ground black pepper.

Transfer to a warmed serving bowl, place in the middle of the table and let everyone help themselves.

SAUTÉED GARLICKY SPINACH

If you're using garden spinach, then you may want to trim off any of the coarser stalks and roughly chop the leaves before you cook it. I find that home-grown leaves can be much larger and altogether more robust than those in a supermarket bag of spinach, so you may need to adjust the cooking time slightly. I like to cook the stalks for a minute or so before adding the leaves, as that gives them a chance to soften before you wilt the leaves.

SERVES 4

45ml/3 tablespoons olive oil
2 garlic cloves, crushed
450g/1lb spinach, washed

Heat the olive oil in a large saucepan over a medium heat, add the garlic and fry for 20 seconds before adding the spinach. Stir to mix the garlic in with the leaves and stir a few more times as the leaves wilt. Add a splash of water if you need to, or cover with a lid and cook for a minute or two until done. Season with sea salt and freshly ground black pepper, then transfer to a warmed serving bowl and serve straight away.

SHAVED COURGETTES WITH BASIL AND MINT

This is a slightly different way of cooking some of those abundant courgettes (zucchini) from the summer veg patch.

SERVES 4

300–350g/10½–12oz courgettes (zucchini)

45ml/3 tablespoons olive oil

2 garlic cloves, finely chopped

zest of 1 lemon

handful of basil leaves, torn

handful of mint leaves, shredded

sea salt

Prepare the courgettes by first topping and tailing them, then slicing them along their length with a vegetable peeler. This will give you long, slim ribbons that will cook very quickly.

Heat the olive oil in a large saucepan over a medium heat, add the garlic and fry for 1 minute until fragrant. Add the courgettes, sprinkle over some sea salt flakes and cook for 4–5 minutes, stirring from time to time. The courgettes are ready when they are soft but still retain some bite. Scatter over the lemon zest, basil and mint leaves and mix once again.

Transfer to a warmed serving bowl and place in the centre of the table.

ROCKET AND SHAVED PARMESAN

Rocket (arugula) has a distinctive peppery flavour, which pairs well with the saltiness of shaved Parmesan cheese. I like to serve this classic salad alongside Rigatoni with Creamy Mushrooms and Crispy Chickpeas (page 108), Spaghetti with Cheesy Marmite Sauce (page 57) or Tagliarini with Cherry Tomatoes and Ricotta (page 68).

SERVES 4

30ml/2 tablespoons olive oil

2 teaspoons balsamic vinegar

150g/5½oz wild rocket (arugula) leaves, rinsed and dried

shaved Parmesan cheese (vegetarian, if necessary), to taste

Pour the olive oil and balsamic vinegar into a large serving bowl and whisk together with a fork before seasoning to taste with sea salt and freshly ground black pepper. Add the rocket and toss together, then scatter over the shaved Parmesan – as much or as little as you like.

VEGAN OPTION

Use Nutritional Yeast (see opposite) instead of the Parmesan.

ROMAINE LETTUCE WITH AVOCADO AND PARMESAN

Catching an avocado at its perfect point of ripeness is a kitchen pleasure. I like to slice them into a crisp Romaine lettuce salad, pairing the soft texture of avocado with the crunchiness of fresh leaves. This salad is good alongside Farfalle with Chorizo and Fig (page 78), Spaghetti with Olives, Anchovies and Rocket (page 106) or Tagliarini with Tuna and Cherry Tomatoes (page 60).

SERVES 4

2 Romaine lettuces

2 avocados, halved and stones removed

30ml/2 tablespoons olive oil

juice of ½ lemon

25g/1oz Parmesan (vegetarian, if necessary), finely grated

Rinse and dry the lettuce leaves, then chop them crossways into 5cm/2in strips. Scoop out the avocado flesh (I like to use a tablespoon to do this in one go), then slice it into bite-sized pieces.

Pour the olive oil and lemon juice into a large serving bowl, whisk together with a fork and season to taste with sea salt and freshly ground black pepper. Add the chopped lettuce and avocado, give everything a good mix and then scatter over the Parmesan before mixing once more.

GREEN BEANS WITH LEMON

This is such a simple way to serve French beans. Olive oil, lemon and Parmesan give a salty-sour lift to what would be quite a plain vegetable dish. They pair well with the strong flavours of olives and anchovies (see Spaghetti with Olives, Anchovies and Rocket, page 106) and tapenade (see Spaghetti alla Tapenade, page 80).

SERVES 4

350g/12oz French beans, tops removed

30ml/2 tablespoons olive oil

zest and juice of ½ lemon

2 tablespoons Nutritional Yeast (see below), or finely grated pecorino or Parmesan, to serve

Bring a medium saucepan of water to the boil before adding salt. Drop the beans into the boiling water and cook for 2–3 minutes; you want them to retain a little bite, so don't cook them until they are soft.

Drain the beans and transfer to a serving bowl. Add the olive oil, lemon zest and juice, mix together and season to taste with sea salt and freshly ground black pepper. Finish by scattering with Nutritional Yeast, pecorino or Parmesan.

NUTRITIONAL YEAST, JAZZED UP

These days, finishing a pasta dish isn't only about Parmesan, pecorino or pangrattato. They may all be traditional, but another good option is nutritional yeast, either on its own or mixed with toasted seeds and nuts. It's full of vitamins, has a nutty umami flavour and is super addictive. Use to sprinkle over pasta dishes, soups and salads; both healthy and delicious.

MAKES 1 SMALL JAR

2 tablespoons pumpkin seeds

2 tablespoons sunflower seeds

2 tablespoons whole almonds

4 tablespoons nutritional yeast

½ teaspoon sea salt flakes

Toast the seeds and nuts in a shallow frying pan (skillet) for around 5–6 minutes until they start turning golden around the edges and the pumpkin seeds begin to pop in the pan. Remove from the heat and transfer to a plate to cool completely, as this allows the nuts to crisp up.

When cool, transfer to a mini chopper or the bowl of a food processor. Blend for 10–15 seconds until you have a texture like coarse sand (it's fine if there are a few chunky pieces). Add the nutritional yeast and the salt, then blend again for a further 5 seconds.

Transfer the mixture to a clean jar and use within a month.

PANGRATTATO

The Italian for breadcrumbs – *pane* is 'bread', *grattugiato* is 'to grate' – *pangrattato* is made with toasted stale bread or the leftover crusts from a loaf and is usually jazzed up with garlic, chilli and herbs. It's a useful, frugal way to use up old bread and create something deliciously crunchy to top off a pasta dish. You can add a variety of extras to the mix – it's up to you, but this is my recipe for a basic pangrattato. You may like to vary the flavour by using different herbs. A few sprigs of picked thyme leaves with the zest of a lemon is lovely and fresh, while a couple of teaspoons of rosemary leaves is a taste of autumn and pairs well with ragù. You will need a food processor or mini chopper for this recipe.

MAKES 1 MEDIUM JAR

4–5 slices of day-old bread

1 small garlic clove

½ teaspoon chilli (hot pepper) flakes

1 generous tablespoon olive oil

sea salt flakes

1 tablespoon chopped parsley

Preheat the oven to 160°C fan/350°F/gas mark 4.

Tear the bread into pieces and arrange these on a baking tray. Place in the oven for 20 minutes. After this time the bread should have toasted nicely and be completely dried out. Don't be hasty and add any olive oil at this stage, as the bread won't stay crisp, which is what you really want. Remove the tray from the oven and allow the bread to cool completely.

Add the cooled bread to the bowl of the food processor or mini chopper along with the remaining ingredients and blitz everything together to make crumbs.

Store the pangrattato in an airtight container – not in the fridge – for up to two weeks. Scatter over soups, salads or any bakes such as cauliflower cheese, as well as using it as a topping for your pasta.

CONFIT GARLIC

In the summer, I often drive the back way home to see if Perwen Farm has any garlic for sale on their roadside stall. I keep a handful of coins ready in the car, so I can drop a couple of pounds into their honesty box and pick up some of their fat, purple-striped garlic. Good-quality, newly harvested garlic makes for excellent confit garlic. The flavour softens and mellows once it's cooked, making it less overpowering than freshly cooked cloves.

Sometimes, just a spoonful of the oil is enough to carry the flavour you would like to add to a dish. Try it in Tagliarini with Basil and Pumpkin Seed Pesto (page 74), Spaghetti with Spinach Sauce (page 66) or Rigatoni with 'No-Vodka Sauce' (page 54).

Use the smallest pan you have for this; you don't want to use loads of expensive olive oil, just enough to cover the garlic.

Confit garlic will keep for up to a month in the fridge, but make sure you sterilize the jar properly and don't let it linger at the back of the shelf for months.

MAKES 1 SMALL JAR

2 heads of garlic, peeled and cloves separated

olive oil, enough to cover

Place the garlic cloves in a small pan, cover them with olive oil and set the pan on a medium heat. Keep an eye on the pan until the olive oil starts bubbling, then reduce the heat to a gentle simmer. The garlic should be cooked and soft after about 25 minutes.

Meanwhile, sterilize a glass jar and its lid. Wash in hot, soapy water, rinse well and then place upside down in the oven at 120°C fan/275°F/gas mark 1 for around 15 minutes.

Once the garlic is cooked, let the pan cool down, then use a slotted spoon to transfer the garlic to the sterilized jar. Carefully pour over the oil, seal with the lid and let the jar fully cool before storing in the fridge.

ABOUT THE AUTHOR

When Mateo first arrived in London from Poland, he had only packed for a two-week trip but ended up taking a job in the kitchen at Mishkin's, a Jewish deli in Soho. Having never set foot in a professional kitchen before and owning only one cookery book – *The Sopranos Family Cookbook*, a present for his seventeenth birthday – a career in the kitchen had never been on the cards, but Mateo felt so at home in the bustling, buzzy atmosphere that he ended up staying to learn all that he could about cooking.

After several years working in a number of restaurants, Mateo is now head chef at 180 Studios in the Strand, a collaborative exhibition, events and media space in central London, where he has been able to create and cook pasta dishes every day. Posting pictures, videos, recipes and tutorials on social media earned him the nickname the Pasta Man, which was the title of his first book, published by Quadrille in 2021. His second book, *Pasta Masterclass*, focused on pasta shaping techniques with accompanying recipes. The making and shaping videos can be found online on the Mateo.Kitchen website.

ACKNOWLEDGEMENTS

I'm extremely lucky to work doing something that I love and I'm grateful to so many people who have encouraged me along the way. It's such a privilege to publish my third cookbook; huge thanks to Sarah Lavelle for suggesting I write another one. I like to call it my Pasta Trilogy.

Publishing a book involves so many people and I'm sure there are dozens behind the scenes whose job it is to get books into readers' hands and in this case into their kitchens. Thank you for all that you do.

To those I've worked with directly on this book, my warmest thanks to:

Publisher Sarah Lavelle, senior editors Kate Burkett and Stacey Cleworth, designer Alicia House, sales director Diana Kojik and all the sales, marketing and publicity team at Quadrille, and to Demeter Scanlon in the USA office. I know I'm in the best hands with such a talented group.

Photographer Matt Russell, master of light, and Claudia Gschwend; what a pleasure to work with you both. Thank you a thousand times over for bringing my food to life on the pages of this book.

Food stylist Katie Marshall, you are always so much fun to work with, making long days in the kitchen fly by.

Charlie Phillips for sourcing the plates and other props, which so reflect the style that I love.

Aldo and Spratt's Factory studio for a beautiful space to work in and for making us feel so at home.

Elizabeth, for everything, always.

180 Studios, for the support of all the team, for giving me the time to be creative in the kitchen and to share what I really love. Thank goodness you are never bored with eating pasta.

All the readers of my books – the home cooks, the pasta makers and followers on social media – it is such a pleasure meeting you, talking with you and sharing my passion for pasta. Please keep posting your pictures and sending your comments to me – it always inspires me to see what you're up to in the kitchen. Enjoy making, sharing and eating your pasta. *Buon appetito* – or *smacznego* – to all of you.

INDEX

Quadrille, Penguin Random House UK, One Embassy Gardens, 8 Viaduct Gardens, London SW11 7BW

Penguin Random House UK

Quadrille Publishing Limited is part of the Penguin Random House group of companies whose addresses can be found at global. penguinrandomhouse.com

Published by Quadrille in 2025

www.penguin.co.uk

A CIP catalogue record for this book is available from the British Library

ISBN 9781837832989

10 9 8 7 6 5 4 3 2 1

Managing Director Sarah Lavelle

Senior Commisisoning Editor Stacey Cleworth

Copy Editor Emily Preece-Morrisson

Proofreader Caroline West

Indexer Cathy Heath

Designer Alicia House

Cover Design Smith & Gilmour

Photographer Matt Russell

Props Stylist Charlie Phillips

Food Stylist Katie Marshall

Production Director Stephen Lang

Production Controller Martina Georgieva

Colour reproduction by F1

Printed in China by C&C Offset Printing Co., Ltd.

The authorised representative in the EEA is Penguin Random House Ireland, Morrison Chambers, 32 Nassau Street, Dublin D02 YH68.

Penguin Random House is committed to a sustainable future for our business, our readers and our planet. This book is made from Forest Stewardship Council® certified paper.

FSC
www.fsc.org
MIX
Paper | Supporting responsible forestry
FSC® C018179